REFORMING
THE ECONOMY

REFORMING THE ECONOMY

JAMES M. RUBUSH

REBUILDING AMERICA

TATE PUBLISHING
AND ENTERPRISES, LLC

Reforming the Economy
Copyright © 2012 by James M. Rubush. All rights reserved.

No part of this publication may be reproduced, stored in a retrieval system or transmitted in any way by any means, electronic, mechanical, photocopy, recording or otherwise without the prior permission of the author except as provided by USA copyright law.

This book is designed to provide accurate and authoritative information with regard to the subject matter covered. This information is given with the understanding that neither the author nor Tate Publishing, LLC is engaged in rendering legal, professional advice. Since the details of your situation are fact dependent, you should additionally seek the services of a competent professional.

The opinions expressed by the author are not necessarily those of Tate Publishing, LLC.

Published by Tate Publishing & Enterprises, LLC
127 E. Trade Center Terrace | Mustang, Oklahoma 73064 USA
1.888.361.9473 | www.tatepublishing.com

Tate Publishing is committed to excellence in the publishing industry. The company reflects the philosophy established by the founders, based on Psalm 68:11,
"The Lord gave the word and great was the company of those who published it."

Book design copyright © 2012 by Tate Publishing, LLC. All rights reserved.
Cover design by Kristen Verser
Interior design by Chelsea Womble

Published in the United States of America

ISBN: 978-1-61862-626-4
1. Education / Finance
2. Business & Economics / Economics / General
12.03.30

This book is dedicated to my daughter, Katherine, in the hopes that by the time she has grandchildren our nation will finally be out of debt. May she grow up to understand things aren't always black and white. She needs to understand the reasons why things are looked at the way they are, and then step back and take a new look as if none of those rules applied. Then figure out how she'd do things differently. May she also understand that laws of nature can't be altered, but laws of man can be changed. By throwing out the laws of man, one can look into changing paradigms and truly create a better world to live in. I also hope she will never settle for the explanation of "that's the way we've always done it."

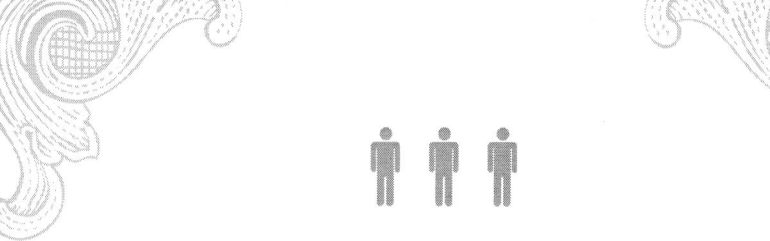

TABLE OF CONTENTS

PREFACE
9

INTRODUCTION
12

COMMON FRAMEWORK TO START FROM
18

TVMEC BASICS
41

TVMEC AND THE THREE PILLARS
OF THE ECONOMY
53

TVMEC VS TAX CUTS
71

ORGANIZATION
81

TVMEC USE IN FOREIGN POLICY
92

FIXING FORECLOSURE LOANS
95

SAVING SOCIAL SECURITY
101

PREVENTING THE MELTDOWN
108

PARTING THOUGHTS
113

REFERENCES
117

PREFACE

This book started as a requirement for my master's thesis in business back in 2003. At the time, I was a major in the United States Air Force, stationed on a one-year remote tour working for NATO in Larissa, Greece. I originally had the basic concept for Time Value of Money Economics floating around inside my head for over a decade, but it wasn't until I actually started putting it down on paper that everything started to click together. Each night as I'd try to sleep, new ideas would just pop up inside my head, I'd get excited, and think about them for hours before getting up and writing them down. Some days, I'd wake up in the morning with only an hour or two of sleep. After a couple of weeks of that, I finally got smart and decided to get a small, digital tape recorder. When I had a new concept worked out in my head, I'd just speak into the recorder and wait until after work the next day to type it into the computer. Although, I eventually received a 100 percent on my paper, I received absolutely no feedback from my professor. For the next seven years, as I continued to expand upon the initial paper, I tried to find a sponsor within the military to help me get my ideas to someone who could do something with them, but I retired in 2010 without any luck.

When my stepfather, Ed Nordmann, passed away in January 2011, I decided I needed to return to my church after going for years as just an "Easter and Christmas" Christian. His sudden passing made me think that I had a lot to give to this world, but the way I was going about it wasn't going to work. On a whim in February 2011, I submitted the manuscript to a publishing company, not knowing if I had a chance to get it published. I'd almost forgotten about submitting it and was asking the Lord to help me make a difference when, later that week, I received the email informing me it was going to be published. It was as if the Lord had answered my prayers. As I was finishing reading the contract, the second to last page came as a shocker to me. It read as a statement of Christian beliefs similar to the Apostle's Creed. To me, it was a sign that I'd made the right choice, both in coming back to church and in choosing this particular publisher. I truly feel blessed that my first attempt at writing a book would be accepted by the first publisher I submitted it to, but more importantly I'll have the opportunity to make the difference I've been looking for.

In addition to God and Tate Publishing, I'd like to thank my wife, Charlotte, and my daughter, Katherine, for their support through the years. Living in a military family and moving every few years isn't easy. I'd also like to thank my dad, Jerry Rubush, for his advice to invest early in life, so it will compound several times before you retire. The insights on the power of compounding money helped form the basis of how to get rid of the national debt. I'd also like to thank my mom, Nancy Nordmann, for her creative example, as well as my sister, Nancy Powers, and brother, Jerry Rubush, for forcing this middle child to learn the art of problem solving to keep the peace. It led me down the path of finding win-win politically-acceptable situations for getting rid of the debt that will help out both the states and citizens while paying off the federal debt in a politically desirable manner.

INTRODUCTION

The US economy, like the Titanic, is huge and looks unstoppable; but it is also very vulnerable if the person at the helm doesn't understand the dangers in the waters ahead and exert the necessary course changes to keep it from sinking. I've been charting these dangers and identifying a path to navigate these waters for the last eight years. A quick explanation of these dangers follows.

In August 2011, US banks were giving out loans with 3.5 percent rates for fixed fifteen-year loans and 4.25 percent for thirty-year fixed loans. The White House and the Congressional Budgeting Office were estimating the US would be paying 5 percent on its ten-year treasury bonds by 2015 and even higher by the end of the decade. Therefore, by 2015 the banks will have to pay its depositors at least 5 percent to keep their money in the banks while receiving only 3.5 percent to 4.25 percent per year over the next fifteen to thirty years on the loans funded by the depositors' money. Obviously, paying out more than you receive isn't fiscally sound and under the current course the government is taking, multiple bailouts will be needed for decades to keep our banking community afloat.

The US has already had 800,000 to 900,000 loans foreclosed upon with another two to three million due to be foreclosed within the next few years. Home prices have already fallen, but are expected to fall another 20 percent over the next two to three years as a result of the additional foreclosures. As the price of the treasury bonds rise, the interest rates charged by banks on new loans will also increase. An increase from 4 percent to 6 percent on a thirty-year loan increases the monthly payments by just over 25 percent. Even though housing prices may be dropping over the next two to three years, the increased interest rates will make them just as unaffordable as they are now. Increased interest rates on adjustable rate mortgages will lead to more foreclosures for those who haven't already converted to a fixed rate mortgage. The current path taken by the government may be stretching out the time period over which these additional foreclosures are enacted, but it's not solving the problem nor will it help. The government needs to enact policies which will help out the people, not just the banks. It needs to address the problem and come up with incentives to keep the homeowners in their houses instead of leaving them with no choice other than to walk away.

Two other groups of people who need to be helped are those currently receiving Social Security and those of us who someday hope there will be something left for us to receive too. Social Security needs to be addressed. It's set up like a pyramid with more people paying in than are receiving. According to the 2011 annual report by the program's board of trustees, 54 million people were receiving Social Security benefits in 2010 while 157 million were paying into the fund (roughly three people paying for each person receiving). Excess money from Social Security payments are invested in US treasury bonds at an artificially low rate of 2 percent (which is below the historic 3 percent rate of inflation) in an effort to keep the average rate paid on treasury bonds lower. The number of people receiving payments from social security is expected to skyrocket as the baby boom generation retires, skewing the ratio of people receiving payments versus the number paying in. It will also consume all the previously accumulated surpluses invested in the US treasury bonds and leave the system bankrupt within the next three decades. If we don't make changes to Social Security now, it'll be an anchor dragging down the economy. We can't afford to keep steering the course on Social Security.

Unfortunately, many Americans also can't afford the cost of a higher education. Education is arguably the single most important factor in increasing an individual's contribution to their society, yet for many Americans higher education is unaffordable. If you don't come from at least a middle class family, even a 1 percent loan can be too costly. For a $60,000 ten-year college loan at a mere 1 percent rate, the monthly payment is over $525. Since it usually takes time to get established in your career field if you don't already have an established network of connections, this $525/month would represent a significant percentage of their monthly income (which is possibly why the default rate is so high on student loans). If the monthly payments could be dropped to as low as $100/month until the person can afford the higher payments, the financial impact of going to college wouldn't be as high, anyone could afford to go to college, and the default rate on the loans would drop. A higher educated person typically earns more money and pays more taxes, which alleviates both state and federal deficits.

Several states (such as California and Illinois) are so far in debt that when their bonds come due they just reissue new bonds to cover the old bond's liabilities, essentially using one credit card to pay off another credit card. By 2015 when the federal government is expected to be paying 5 percent on its treasury bonds, these state governments will be forced to pay even higher rates since their bonds are less secure than federal bonds. This will translate into either higher taxes just to provide the same level of services or a reduction in services provided by the state. Either way, it will hurt the state's economy. How far into debt must the federal government allow the states to go before it provides relief?

The federal debt is skyrocketing out of control. The politicians can't agree on what to do. They keep debating over whether they should cut spending or raise taxes. What they're not doing is looking for other ways to raise revenues which will solve their economic problems while balancing the budget and paying off the national debt.

These are just some of the topics this book will recommend solutions to. Each solution is designed with win-win scenarios in mind to help the individual taxpayer save money, the economy to recover, and the government to earn new revenue without raising taxes. The basic premise is the government prints up money and loans the money out, using the accounts receivable on the loans both as an asset to balance its books against (so it doesn't need to issue more treasury bonds) and as a mechanism to pull the money back out of the economy by destroying the loans' principal as it's paid back. This mechanism to return the money supply back to normal is in stark contrast to the current policy of "monetizing" the debt where the government just prints up money and uses it to buy its own debt, essentially devaluating the dollar with no mechanism to restore the dollar's value later on. As an additional check on inflationary pressures, the plan takes advantage of the increase in the tax base caused by increasing the money supply. In a perfect society, if we printed up $300 billion our tax base would also increase by $300 billion and we'd be able to get the whole $300 billion back in taxes. I'm using a conservative estimate that we'd only get 2/3 of that back. When we get that additional $200 billion in taxes at the end of the year, I'm advocating destroying it immediately. This would decrease inflationary pressures caused by printing up the money in the first place, decrease any devaluation of the dollar, and create a huge insurance policy (67 percent) against defaults on the loans. Since we've printed up and loaned out $300 billion and we've already destroyed $200 billion of the printed money when we received it back in the form of additional taxes, we only need to destroy $100 billion worth of the principal we receive on these $300 billion in loans to restore the money supply to normal. The other $200 billion in principal would be available as additional revenue for the federal government.

COMMON FRAMEWORK TO START FROM

Any discussion of economic basics would be remiss if it didn't start with a discussion of the Law of Supply and Demand. To understand the Law of Supply and Demand, you must first understand what a market is. A market is "a group of individuals and/or organizations that have needs for products in a product class and have the ability, willingness, and authority to purchase those products."[1]—basically the people who want, can, and will buy a product. If individuals don't have needs for the product or the authority to buy it, they won't purchase them regardless of the price. The other two factors, ability and willingness, are subject to change and form the basis for the Law of Supply and Demand. A fixed number of customers exist who have the need, ability, willingness, and authority to buy a product at a given price. If the price is increased, fewer people will have the ability to purchase it, and others who still have the ability may change their mind and no longer want to buy it at the new price. If the price is decreased, more people will have the ability to buy the product, and others who previously had the ability may change their mind and buy it. This represents the Law of Demand where more people will purchase a product at a lower price, while fewer will purchase it at a higher price. Of course, there are exceptions to the rule. For luxury items, a lower price can be seen as lower quality and lead to lower demand. The Law of Supply is similar, only it deals with the providers of the product. More producers have the ability to supply a product at a higher price. GM can't afford to sell a car for one dollar, but it can for twenty thousand dollars. They also have the willingness to supply products at a higher price and therefore the supply of a product is increased at a higher price, while the opposite holds true for a lower price. In theory, the point where supply and demand intersects determines the sustainable price for a product. In reality, the company will determine the price at which it can maximize profit with the current demand for the product and sell at that price. If either the supply or the demand changes, the new point where profit can be maximized determines the price. This combination of the two is called the Law of Supply and Demand.

Now that we understand the Law of Supply and Demand, I'd like to explain the cause of inflation, but before I can adequately explain the cause of inflation, I must explain discretionary income. Income is how much total money is earned before taxes. Disposable income is "the amount of money left after payment of taxes."[2] Discretionary income is "disposable income available for spending and saving after an individual has purchased the basic necessities of food, clothing, and shelter."[3] Consumers use discretionary income to buy all of their "wants." A change in discretionary income alters a consumer's ability and willingness to buy products, and therefore affects the demand curve for products. A change in discretionary income can be the result of a change in total income; a change in the costs of food, clothing, or shelter; or as a result of a change in the tax rate—all three will alter discretionary income. If the average household's discretionary income is increased, there will be an increased demand for most products. In this situation, the law of supply and demand would dictate that suppliers would be able to increase their prices and still produce or sell the same number of goods. This generalized increase in the average costs of goods is called inflation.

Due to inflation, a dollar today won't be worth a dollar tomorrow, even though it's still a dollar. This brings us to the time value of money. If an item costs one dollar today, and the inflation rate is 3 percent, it would take $1.03 to buy the same item next year. This loss of buying power is what many people think of when referring to the time value of money, but a second half of the equation also exists. A dollar today can be invested and be worth more than a dollar tomorrow. Most people won't invest their money unless the rate of return on their investment is greater than the rate of inflation, otherwise they'd lose buying power with their money, and it would make more sense to spend it today, instead. However, if a person invests one dollar today at a rate of return of 5 percent and inflation is 3 percent, the investor will have $1.05 next year and can buy the item that would then cost $1.03 and still have two cents left over. In this case, both the value of the investor's money and his buying power have increased. I'm using a combination of the two as the basis for paying off the federal debt. What if you could borrow a dollar today, pay no interest, loan the dollar out, and wait ten years to pay it back? Even if you loaned it out at less then the rate of inflation, both you and the person borrowing from you would be in a win-win situation. If it were the government instead of you loaning that dollar out, and you were the one borrowing at less than the rate of inflation, the interest you paid the government could be used to stimulate the economy or pay off a part of the federal debt while the money you borrowed would provide you with new economic opportunities at a lower cost. With a recession going on, we could definitely use that stimulus to the economy, but where should it be applied?

Education, infrastructure, and investment capital are the three pillars of our economy which need to be strengthened if we are going to pull out of this recession. Education determines the technological level our workers are able to support, as well as the number of innovations invented each year to develop and sustain future economic growth. Infrastructure provides the means to produce the goods as well as the ability to get the goods to the consumers who will buy them. Investment capital provides the fiscal ability to take advantage of the ideas innovators develop by providing the resources necessary to transform their ideas into reality and creates future economic growth. Ending the recession and maintaining a healthy economy requires a balance among the three. If the level of education produces more innovative opportunities than the level of investment capital can support, people will take their ideas overseas and sell them where the opportunity exists to profit from them. If more investment capital is available than what's required for funding current innovations, investors will invest their money in areas overseas where the opportunities exist and capital isn't available. Infrastructure improvements require innovative ideas as well as investment capital to fund the projects, and in return provide jobs and reduce the cost of getting goods to market. The right combination of the three will produce sustainable opportunities for future economic growth. The following is an excerpt from the Congressional Budget Office's "Analysis of the Presidents Budget Program for 2004" and provides a good summary of supply-side and demand-side economics:

> The aggregate production of goods and services changes over time in two distinct ways. First, the economy's underlying potential to generate output rises with increases in the quantity and quality of the labor force, the size of the stock of productive capital, and the level of technological know-how. Economists refer to those three determinants of potential output as "supply-side" variables because they determine the quantity of goods and services that the

> economy is capable of supplying. Supply-side changes have a lasting effect on the economy.
>
> Second, actual economic output cycles around its potential level, as unemployment rises and falls and the stock of capital is used more or less intensively. Those movements are referred to as demand-side, or cyclical, variations because they occur as the total demand for goods and services moves above and below the level of potential output. Unlike movements in the supply side of the economy, cyclical changes are temporary—built-in corrective forces tend to move the economy back toward the potential level determined by the supply side.
>
> When the economy is below its potential level of output, policies that increase aggregate demand can increase output without running the risk of accelerating inflation.

What gems can we gleam from supply and demand side economics to improve the three pillars of the economy? Investing in higher education will improve both the quantity and quality of the workforce. The quantity will increase as functionally obsolete workers retrain for new skills and the level of technical know-how will increase as the educational level of the average worker rises. Investing in infrastructure improvements lowers the costs of getting goods to market and makes companies more competitive. Supply side economics tells us these are the types of improvements which will have a lasting effect on the economy. On the demand side, increasing the amount of investment capital available will increase economic output and reduce unemployment. Since the economy is below its potential economic level during recessionary times, increasing the money supply with additional investment capital will have a minimal effect on inflation while providing for immediate economic growth.

Now that we know about the way the three pillars interact with the economy, why do we sometimes have recessions, and why do we need fiscal deficits? As mentioned above, actual economic output cycles around its potential level, as unemployment rises and falls and the stock of capital is used more or less intensively and these changes are caused as the total demand for goods and services moves above and below the level of potential output. The CBO also stated that cyclical changes are temporary—built-in corrective forces tend to move the economy back toward the potential level determined by the supply side, but what happens when the supply side is out of balance? If the supply side is out of balance, such as when the amount of investment capital is reduced and unemployment rises, the economy might not be able to recover without help. When unemployment rises, fewer people are able to buy goods, companies respond by producing less and laying more people off, the government's tax revenues decrease, and the government would be forced to reduce services or lay people off if it were to maintain a balanced budget. This slowing down of the economy longer than a normal cycle is called a recession. If the government doesn't step in to bring the economy back into balance, we could end up with another Great Depression. In the Great Depression, investment capital wasn't available, a relatively large portion of the population was without jobs, and fewer people were paying taxes—all because the government was pursuing laissez-faire economics and thought the economy would take care of itself. During recessions, it takes an additional stimulus to get the economy back on track and this stimulus comes through the government spending more than it receives in revenues, causing a federal deficit.

Now, we're ready to discuss the federal debt. What is the federal debt? At the end of each fiscal year (October 1 to September 30), the government balances its books and determines if it has a fiscal surplus or a fiscal deficit for the year. The results for the fiscal year are added to the accumulated results of all previous years to determine the total value of the Federal Surplus or Federal Debt. In other words, the US Federal Debt that we have now is the accumulated total of the results of all previous fiscal surpluses and fiscal deficits since the founding of the United States.

When the US government spends more money than it has and therefore has a federal deficit or debt, how does it get the rest of the funds to pay its bills? The US government borrows the money from investors. If the loan is for one year or less, it's called a treasury bill. If the loan is for two to five years, it's called a treasury note. Finally, if the loan is for greater than five years, it's called a treasury bond. The government auctions off its debt to investors and uses the money received to pay its bills. These auctions are subject to the law of supply and demand with the investors setting the supply of money available for each increment of interest and the government determining the demand. If the government doesn't have enough money to pay the debt when the loans (treasury bills, notes, or bonds) come due, it rolls over the debt by issuing new treasury bills, treasury notes, and treasury bonds to pay the bill. One way of looking at it is the government is doing the equivalent of taking out a cash advance with a credit card to pay another credit card. Although the government can continue rolling over the debt for as long as there are investors willing to loan the government money at the going interest rate, rolling over the debt affects the demand curve.

When the government rolls over the federal debt into new loans, current year fiscal deficits must compete with the rolled over federal debt for investment money. The total demand for investor's money is increased, which results in a higher interest rate required for meeting both the fiscal deficit and the federal debt. Due to the nature of the supply curve, this higher interest rate must be greater than the expected rate of inflation during the period of the loan. If the interest rate is lower than the expected rate of inflation, investors won't invest their money, because they'd lose buying power. Although this relationship between interest rates and inflation is a near absolute for the public sector's investments, it doesn't always hold true for the government sector's investments.

Two uniquely distinguishable sectors invest in the markets for treasury bills, notes, and bonds. The first sector is the public sector. Individuals and institutions with excess savings that they intend to invest in a low risk investment providing a return on their investments greater than the rate of inflation generally characterize this sector. They follow the general rule that slow and steady will win the race and want a guaranteed income in the future. As of March 16, 2011, the public sector holds $9,619,622,421,602.38 out of the total federal debt of $14,232,849,993,955.10[4]. The second sector is the government sector. The government sector is composed of a variety of government funds with the majority investment funds being the Federal Old-Age and Survivors Insurance Trust Fund (Social Security) with over $2 trillion, the Civil Service Retirement and Disability Fund with about $1 trillion, the Federal Hospital Insurance Trust Fund with over $300 billion, the Department of Defense Military Retirement Fund with over $200 billion, and the Federal Disability Insurance Trust Fund also with over $200 billion.[5] The total value of the government sector is $4,613,227,572,352.72.[6] Many of these funds, such as the Social Security Trust Fund, are required by law to invest its surplus funds in treasury bills, notes, and bonds regardless of the interest rate earned.

Why would the government require the government's funds to invest in treasury bills, notes, and bonds? By requiring these governmental funds to invest in these instruments, the government affects the demand curve. If the governmental funds didn't invest in these instruments, the public sector would have to come up with the rest of the money, or the government couldn't pay its bills. To get investors to come up with the additional money, the government would have to offer a higher rate to counter its higher demand for investor's funds. Therefore, by requiring the governmental funds to invest in treasury bills, notes, and bonds, the government reduces the rate of interest it pays on all of these instruments and saves money. As a result of requiring the governmental funds to buy the debt at the 2 percent rate, interest payments on the debt in 2010 averaged only 2.9 percent.

All the money the government has received for all the pension funds, including social security, has already been spent. There is no physical cash left to pay it back, only an entry in the debt logs of how much it owes. Since I originally started writing this eight years ago as my master's thesis paper, the amount owned by the government sector has increased by two trillion dollars. For all intensive purposes, the government might have just as well increased your taxes by that amount, because the only way it will be able to pay it back is through additional taxes under the current system. The government's used the surplus from the other governmental funds to buy treasury bonds because it was the only way it could raise the funds needed to cover its debt. Last year, Social Security payments exceeded the amount, coming in through Social Security taxes by $37 billion, so the government will no longer be able to finance its debt through the extra money previously received when Social Security taxes exceeded social security payments. In fact, it will have to borrow additional money now to meet its social security payments. As a result, the overall rate paid on the debt will rise for two reasons. First, Social Security will no longer be a source of funds, so other investors will have to be enticed with a higher rate of interest to cover the normal debt payments. Secondly, the amount of investment money needed will further increase to cover the portion of Social Security payments not covered by Social Security taxes received during the year. This is one of the reasons why the Congressional Budgeting Office is projecting it will have to pay 5 percent interest by 2015 and more by the end of the decade.

How long can the government keep borrowing money and rolling over its debt? The answer to the question is "it depends." Everything is relative. Standard and Poor's just recently downgraded the US's debt rating.[7] This could increase the cost of borrowing money if another currency were to be seen as more stable than the dollar. We recently flirted with this possibility becoming reality in August 2011 when political posturing between the Democrats and Republicans almost led to a default on our loans, but we held off the default with some last minute compromises to form a bilateral super-committee to resolve the differences. In the meantime, when people look at whether or not to invest in a government's bonds, some people compare the size of the federal debt to the nation's Gross Domestic Product (GDP). The most recent calculation for the United States' GDP was $14.58 trillion.[8] This would mean that the ratio of federal debt ($14.23 trillion) to GDP is currently 0.978. In Aug 2008, it was only 0.668. The United States all-time historic high for this ratio was 1.14 at the end of World War II.[9] This would lead to speculation that the federal debt could still increase in relation to GDP, and under the right economic conditions the United States could recover from that much debt. But would investors be able to come up with that much money? During the 1980s, according to economist Benjamin M. Friedman, borrowing by the federal government to finance its debt absorbed almost 75 percent of all net savings by American citizens and businesses.[10] Borrowing by the federal government has only increased since then. With the percentage of debt to GDP increasing as fast as it has, the public sector can't afford to keep taking its capital investment money and investing it in the debt without damaging the economy. Financing this much debt now requires heavy investment from foreign markets and leaves little, if any, net savings for growth (both domestically and to some extent in the foreign market). "Monetizing the debt"—printing up money to buy our own debt—has led to a 20 percent devaluation of the dollar against our primary trading partners over the last decade as we water down our currency. Since our ten-year treasury bills are now paying only 2 percent a year, we can't continue to monetize the debt and expect foreigners to still invest in our economy. The entire 20 percent they'd earn in interest over the ten-year period would be wiped out when they converted the dollars back into their currency. If we continue to monetize the debt, we'll be forced to offer substantially higher interest rates to attract foreign investors. The higher rates will also translate into higher debt payments requiring more investment capital to be diverted to paying our nation's loans. Without investment capital for growth, our economy would slowly disintegrate with higher federal deficits (due to slower or negative growth) leading to a spiraling federal debt in a vicious cycle.

Other economists compare the amount of money spent on interest payments to the GDP of the nation. In 2010, the United States spent $413,954,825,362.17 on interest payments for its debt.[11] Comparatively speaking, the United States interest payment as a percentage of overall GDP (2.84 percent) is smaller than the same ratios for other developed countries, so the

United States should have no problems rolling over its debt. Once again, though, this can be misleading, because the government is not truly limited by the amount of interest it can pay, but by the amount of debt that can be financed. Also, the interest payment as a percentage of overall GDP has grown by 40 percent over the last fifteen years. This isn't a good trend and it's not expected to get any better. According to the Congressional Budget Office's Analysis of the President's Budgetary Proposals for Fiscal Year 2011, "debt held by the public would grow from $7.5 trillion (53 percent of GDP) at the end of 2009 to $20.3 trillion (90 percent of GDP) at the end of 2020 and net interest would grow to 4.1 percent in 2020."[12] This change in percentage is partially due to Social Security no longer having a surplus and the need for the public to takeover it's portion of the debt. If the public sector is really expected to come up with an additional $12.8 trillion by 2020 and invest it in our national debt, will anything be left to invest in our economy?

What does the federal debt have to do with economic growth? As mentioned earlier, the public sector has invested about 75 percent of its net savings in financing the federal debt and "as a result, gross private domestic investment appears to have declined as a share of GDP."[13] "That's why the federal debt is frequently characterized as consuming the 'seed corn' we should be planting in the form of productive investments for the future."[14] This redirection of investment capital has effectively applied a brake to the economy compared to how large it could have been had there been no federal debt and if all the net savings had been applied toward financing the economy instead. In comparison, the world economy has experienced an overall slowing down in its growth, or even a recession in many places. Whether or not it can be attributed to the amount of money spent on financing the US debt doesn't matter at this point. What does matter is getting out of this recession will take an increase in spending. Under the current economic system, this can be done in two ways—increased government spending or cutting taxes to increase discretionary income. If such a large percentage of net savings is still tied up in the deficit, personal spending can't be relied upon to increase significantly without further tax cuts so the government needs to step in.

Increased government sector spending would result in a stimulus to the current economy and increased tax revenue (because most of the money spent would be on taxable items or income), but there are outflows of money from our economy, such as trade deficits. Due to these outflows, not every dollar of increased government spending will be received back in taxes. Each dollar lost due to those outflows from the increased government sector spending will require a dollar of investment capital to be taken out of the economy to finance it. If the reason for the recession is a lack of investment capital, this could aggravate the situation.

Instead of increasing government spending, the government could decrease taxes to stimulate the economy. Decreasing taxes to increase private sector spending frees up capital for personal consumption or savings by increasing discretionary income. Some people will use these tax savings for buying luxury items they previously hadn't budgeted for. Other people will use the tax savings to pay off current credit card or bank loans. This frees up investment capital for other people or companies that need it and can lead to future technological breakthroughs and economic growth. Still other people will invest directly in mutual funds or in stocks which they feel will outperform the economy. This directly leads to future economic growth if the stocks invested in are new upstart companies, or companies that continually strive for better products such as 3M or GE. Using tax cuts also means taking in less tax revenue, which means having a higher federal deficit, unless the tax cut is also accompanied by a decrease in the government sector spending. Unfortunately, cutting government sector spending would also reduce the impact of the tax cuts. The problem with always using tax cuts to overcome recessions is that eventually the tax rates are so low that the law of diminishing returns will set in. Eventually, you'll arrive at the point where cutting taxes won't lead to enough additional capital spending and growth to compensate for the decreased tax revenues and the increased deficit resulting from the tax cuts. For instance, if you cut the tax rate from 20 percent of income to 19 percent of income, you give the taxpayers 1 percent of their income back while reducing tax revenues by 5 percent. If you continue to use this method, eventually you will be reducing taxes from 2 percent to 1 percent to give the taxpayer the same 1 percent of income back while reducing revenues by 50 percent. Even though that money will be spent many more times before becoming consumed by taxes, eventually there's a limit to how many times money can change hands within a year (as well as greater cumulative losses from the economy due to outflows each time it's spent), making it impossible to receive it all back within a single fiscal cycle and reducing annual revenue. Obviously, using only this method for overcoming recessions can't be sustained indefinitely.

Before I can introduce you to a new tool for overcoming recessions, I need to introduce one last economic item—the money supply. When talking about the money supply in reference to the economy, I'm referring to the M1 money supply that's instantly available for potential investment purposes.

> The narrowest definition of the money stock in common use by the advanced industrial countries today ("M1") includes only the paper currency and coinage in circulation among the public plus the total balances instantly available to depositors in privately held checking accounts ("demand deposits" or "sight deposits") in the country's commercial banks and similar depository institutions (like savings and loans, credit unions, etc.). (A very large proportion of checking account money, of course, is simply created by the banks themselves as they extend loans to borrowers by simply crediting their borrowers' checking account balances with the amounts loaned). Travelers' checks are also included in M1 in some countries, including the US.[15]

The money supply is an important item when it comes to investment capital and economic growth. An increase in the money supply can provide an increase in investment capital, as well as an increase in economic growth, as more capital leads to more spending; but it can also lead to greater inflation. A decrease in money supply can lead to a decrease in investment capital and potentially to a recession. According to the 2000 report from the US Trade Deficit Review Commission, outflows of money from our economy through the "large and growing U.S. trade and current account deficits also pose a threat to the health of the domestic economy. This led us to question the sustainability of the trade deficit."[16] How much of a problem is it? "Imbalances in international accounts persisted during 2006 with the trade deficit at about 6 percent of GDP and the current account deficit at nearly 7 percent of GDP."[17] The current account deficit represents not only the trade deficit, but also what foreigners invest in the US versus what we invest in their countries. At the end of 2006, foreign holdings of Treasury debt were $2.134 trillion, which was 44 percent of the total debt held by the public at that time.[18] "The increase in foreign holdings was 86 percent of total federal borrowing in 2006 and about 72 percent of total federal borrowing over the last four years."[19] What this means is our trade deficits are being reinvested in our debt.

Under normal market conditions (without an ever expanding federal debt) if the United States had a trade deficit, the value of the dollar would drop making our goods cheaper overseas, their goods more expensive in the United States, and the trade deficit would change to a trade surplus as we sold more and bought less. This process would go back and forth with economic activity and growth cycling along with the trade deficits and surpluses. With the ever expanding federal debt, this cycle has been disrupted. Instead of the foreigners buying our goods, they're now reinvesting the dollars back in our debt and keeping the currency rates the same while perpetuating the trade deficit. This keeps their economies strong. Although the capital infusion into our debt keeps our government solvent, the constant outflow of money also forces our government to keep overspending in order to avoid a recession. To get out of this cycle, we have two options. The first is to reduce our spending on foreign goods. With a populace that is marginally educated at best in economics, this would be a tough sell politically to get them to change their habits and also understand that the value of the dollar would need to drop before things would get better. We'd also have to worry about any "Buy American" program ticking off the foreigners to the point where they'd stop investing or pull their money out of our debt, thereby bankrupting the government. The other option is to come up with a new approach to economics that would not only provide the additional revenue needed to prevent annual deficits, but also pay off the federal debt. I've come up with that new approach and I call it Time Value of Money Economics (TVMEC).

TVMEC BASICS

When I first came up with the idea for TVMEC in 2003, I was looking for a way to make the Social Security system solvent in the future when the outflows of money would exceed what's coming in. I was going to need an infusion of cash when none existed. Since all the Social Security system's funds were tied up in treasury bonds, I decided to modify the way the government currently uses treasury bonds and social security payments. The key to TVMEC in this situation was allowing the purchaser of the treasury bonds to put down a fraction of the original bond value up front and pay the rest of the money at a later date. The government would temporarily print up new money to make up the difference and when the principal is paid on the due date, it would be destroyed, resulting in a "bubble" of expanded money supply but a "net zero increase" over the long term. The "bubble" would be earning interest with the majority of the pay back being toward the far end of the time stream. This allows the interest to compound, and pay off not only all the printed money in the bubble and its underlying debt, but to provide extra money for balancing the budget as well. This process requires a determination of how much money can be printed without adversely affecting the economy with inflation, an incentive higher than what's currently available for investors, a future-weighted payback schedule that guarantees investors will pay the money back at the due date, and a congressional mandate to destroy the money after it's turned back in.

The Federal Reserve Board or a similar government organization should estimate the first item—a determination of how much money can be printed without adversely affecting the money supply with inflation. Back in 2003, I recommended using President Bush's Tax Cut as a guide. I did so because the amount of money it released had already been determined and tax cuts increase discretionary spending just like printing money and loaning it out does. Recently, I've changed my mind to reflect the current loan debacle where over $700 billion was injected into the economy. I decided instead to inject $300 billion each year for two years before stabilizing the economy at a new money supply level ($600 billion higher than it currently is). Other possible starting points include either the trade deficit or the deficit for the current account balance. They both give lagging indications as to the outflows of money from the economy, and those amounts of cash infusions would be needed if foreigners were no longer investing in our debt while we still had a trade imbalance. Items to consider include the state of the economy; fewer opportunities would exist for foreign investment in our debt, so portions of the trade deficit may stay overseas as the debt gets paid off before coming back in the form of a trade surplus; and the trend of the late 1990s when more people started investing in global mutual funds.

The second item, an incentive for investors, is created by the opportunities afforded by allowing them to place only a portion of the money down initially. This lets them receive interest on the full value of the bond while investing the rest of the money elsewhere. For example, if I have $1,000 to invest, I can buy a ten-year treasury bond, paying 2 percent interest, and I only have to put down ten percent (which equals $100) for the first nine years. I can invest the other $900 for the next nine years and earn a return on that $900 investment at the same time. The government would print up $900 to cover the amount given back, and when I put down the other $900 after nine years, the government would destroy the original money it had printed up to cover that $900. For the net of $100 invested, after receiving the other $900 back that I had put down to cover the $1,000 note, I'd earn $20 in interest the first year alone. That $20 return on a $100 investment is the equivalent of earning 20 percent interest. Why would the government be willing to do this? The government is only paying 2 percent interest on the entire $1,000 note—less than half of the projected ten-year treasury bond rate (see Table 1).

TABLE 1: FORECASTED TEN-YEAR TREASURY NOTE RATES

Actual	Forecast	Projected Annual Averages		
2010	2011	2012	2013-2016	2017-2021
3.2	3.4	3.8	4.7	5.4

Source: An Analysis of the President's Budgetary Proposals for the Fiscal Year 2011

The third item, a future-weighted pay-back schedule guaranteeing investors will pay the money back at the due date, is an extension of the second item. How do you guarantee the money will be paid back at the due date? The answer is by keeping the money in the system the entire time. You tier down the offerings to the investor in a cascading effect. The investor is required to invest the $900 given back to him on a nine-year $900 Treasury bond and, in return, the government prints up and gives him back $800 for eight years. He's then required to invest that $800 on an eight-year treasury bond and the government then prints up and gives him $700 back. The process continues on down the line to the final one-year, $100 treasury bill. The process is future-weighted because the majority of the printed money is due to be paid back at the end of the period. The government prints up the extra needed at each stage of the tier and destroys the printed portion when it's paid back. When the one-year treasury bill comes due, the principal is applied toward the two-year treasury note, bringing its principal back up to $200. When the two-year treasury bill comes due, its principal is applied to the three-year treasury bill and so on, guaranteeing the money will be available when it's due. The investor doesn't get to keep the principal for the printed up money (it's destroyed when paid to get rid of the bubble), only the interest from the money printed for the tiered down bonds. Table 2 illustrates the basic compounding power for the tiered down example mentioned above. The table starts at Year zero with the various tiered down amounts from $1,000 down to $100 in the first row. Each of those amounts earns 2 percent interest at the end of the first year, so the amounts change for the Year one row. Note that the Year one row only shows $2 in its $100 column. That's because the one-year $100 Treasury note has come due and the $100 printed up for that note was now rolled up into the two-year $200 Treasury note, leaving only the earned interest behind. During the second year, the new amounts earn 2 percent interest and at the end of the second year we roll up the $200 amount into the $300 Treasury note. The process continues each year until the ten-year Treasury bond comes due at the end of ten years. If we hadn't tiered down the money, the investor's $1,000 would only have grown to $1,218.99 as shown at the bottom of the $1,000 column. Since we did tier it down, the $1,000 invested also earned the additional compounded interest amounts shown at the bottom of the other columns and the total grew to $1,860.89. Even though the government is still paying only a 2 percent rate on any of the money covered, the overall yield increasing from $1,218.99 to $1,860.89 corresponds to a 6.4 percent effective rate for the $1,000 put down by the investor. Longer loan durations allow for more tiers and more time for money to compound before the printed money is due to be destroyed. The example above replaced the need for additional investment capital to buy Treasury bonds by using the printed money to magnify the initial investment to cover more bonds and fill the gap, but it didn't pay off the underlying debt. Longer durations will actually provide the capability to both increase the effective rate and pay off the underlying debt. TVMEC is fulfilling the need for investors to obtain higher rates of return on their money while keeping the government's debt payments from spiraling out of control.

TABLE 2: ILLUSTRATION OF THE TIERED DOWN EFFECT

Year	Amount										
0	$1,000.00	$900.00	$800.00	$700.00	$600.00	$500.00	$400.00	$300.00	$200.00	$100.00	
1	$1,020.00	$918.00	$816.00	$714.00	$612.00	$510.00	$408.00	$306.00	$204.00	$2.00	
2	$1,040.40	$936.36	$832.32	$728.28	$624.24	$520.20	$416.16	$312.12	$8.08	$2.04	
3	$1,061.21	$955.09	$848.97	$742.85	$636.72	$530.60	$424.48	$18.36	$8.24	$2.08	
4	$1,082.43	$974.19	$865.95	$757.70	$649.46	$541.22	$32.97	$18.73	$8.41	$2.12	
5	$1,104.08	$993.67	$883.26	$772.86	$662.45	$52.04	$33.63	$19.10	$8.57	$2.16	
6	$1,126.16	$1,013.55	$900.93	$788.31	$75.70	$53.08	$34.30	$19.49	$8.75	$2.21	
7	$1,148.69	$1,033.82	$918.95	$104.08	$77.21	$54.14	$34.99	$19.88	$8.92	$2.25	
8	$1,171.66	$1,054.49	$137.33	$106.16	$78.76	$55.23	$35.69	$20.27	$9.10	$2.30	
9	$1,195.09	$175.58	$140.07	$108.28	$80.33	$56.33	$36.40	$20.68	$9.28	$2.34	
10	$1,218.99	$179.09	$142.88	$110.45	$81.94	$57.46	$37.13	$21.09	$9.47	$2.39	$1,860.89
	Original Interest Rate = 2%, Effective Interest Rate = 6.4%										

The government is already facing budgetary pressures to cut spending and increase taxes, so it can't afford to pay over 2 percent on its loans. Keeping the interest payments down will be next to impossible on the path we're currently on. With payments out of Social Security exceeding what's coming in, the government is no longer able to invest its excess payments in the US treasury bonds because there is no excess. Instead, the government has to borrow even more money to cover the Social Security deficit. Investors will require a higher return to meet this higher demand for their money. Tiering the payments as mentioned will meet the needs of both groups by allowing the government to continue to pay only a fixed 2 percent rate while providing the investor with the greater return on investment (6.4 percent) they'd require. As the government continues to convert all its treasury bonds over to these tiered bonds, it would reduce the current 2.9 percent average rate it's paying now down to 2 percent; reducing its debt payments and (by extension) reducing its annual deficits as well. The effective rate could also be lowered to less than 2 percent by having the tiered down bonds pay less than 2 percent, and the yield would still be competitive in the market place through TVMEC.

Why do we need a future-heavy schedule for paying back the printed money? So the time value of money can be applied and the interest can be compounded. An illustration of the future-heavy pay back schedule's advantages can be seen by comparing the effects of using TVMEC versus what would happen if the government just printed up the money and then paid back/destroyed $100 billion a year for one hundred years (see Figure 1). You'll notice in the figure that the amount of debt the government is able to pay off in this manner steadily climbs by $100 billion/year until Year one hundred. After Year one hundred, no residual effect exists so the amount stays constant at $10 trillion paid off. The slope of the tiered TVMEC line is constantly increasing, reflecting the compounding interest. Even after Year one hundred when all the money has been printed up, the slope continues to increase, reflecting that by Year one hundred five times more money is capable of being paid off per year due to compounding interest ($513B) than was even being printed up ($100B). The tiered TVMEC system is able to pay off $29.3 trillion of debt by Year one hundred, $69.8 trillion worth by Year 150, and $172 trillion by year 200 when the last of the money that was printed during the initial one hundred years is paid back. This is the kind of power TVMEC is harnessing through the compounding of interest even at a mere 2 percent rate.

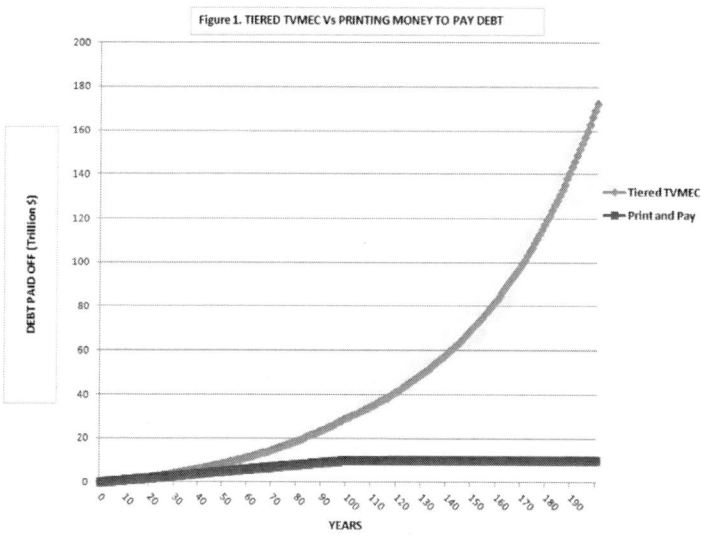

The final item required for TVMEC to work is a congressional mandate to destroy the money after it's turned back in. This is not just a moral argument necessary for accountability and to prevent abuses (as well as keep faith in our currency), but a critical part of preventing hyperinflation. Failure to destroy the money leads to devaluation of our currency. Under our current practice of "Monetizing the Debt," the US has been printing up money to buy our debt without taking that money back out. As a result, the value of the US dollar has dropped by an average of 20 percent over the last ten years against our top ten trading partners. The dollar is currently the world's standard because of its stability. However, if we continue to flood the markets with printed up money without a mechanism to take that money back out and the dollar continues to drop, we risk people losing faith in the dollar's stability. This would lead to higher interest rates required to get foreign investors to buy our treasury bills because investors would think twice before they'd convert their currency into dollars to buy our ten year treasury bonds if they knew they'd lose over 20 percent of their investment when they convert their money back. Yet this is exactly the path we're currently following with our monetary policy. As long as we can show we'll destroy all the money printed up and our money supply will return to normal at a known date in the future, the value of the dollar will recover and the value of their investment is safe. That's why we need a Congressional mandate to destroy the money when it comes due.

At this point, I'd like to point out an important difference between printing up money responsibly through TVMEC and lowering the tax rate to stimulate the economy. When you print up money, you actually increase the money supply, which increases the tax base. In a perfect closed system, if you printed up $300 billion, you'd receive it all back in new taxes…allowing you to spend more or to decrease the size of any deficit you currently have. What I'm suggesting is to print up the $300 billion for the first three years and allow the money supply to expand by a total of $600 billion. In the third and subsequent years when the extra tax revenue (above the $600 billion level) comes in, it should be destroyed, and the amount should be written off from what needs to be destroyed when the principal comes in from the loans. This would provide a much needed stimulus to our economy. Although I'm not an advocate of raising taxes, if the politicians in power decide not to extend the Bush era tax cuts, the introduction of TVMEC could offset the economic consequences. Normally, once tax cuts are initiated, they can't be rescinded without causing a recession because the economy has already adjusted to the higher level of discretionary income spending and raising taxes cuts discretionary spending. The inflationary pressures caused during the first two years of TVMEC when the money supply is expanded would help counteract the recessionary pressures caused by the sunsetting of the tax cuts. If needed, the introduction of TVMEC could even be slowed to match the sunsetting of the tax cuts, but it would be doubtful whether that level of spending would be enough to seriously mitigate or end our current recessionary trend. Since unemployment is high, introducing TVMEC at this time would have minimal inflationary effects even without sunsetting the tax cuts. Companies have excess infrastructure and office space being unused due to layoffs. As a result, a stimulus like TVMEC that increases the economic activity level won't cause a large increase in the costs of producing more goods as more workers are hired to take on the additional workload. Initially, the additional workers will use the existing space and currently unused equipment and bring the company back up to its optimum level. This will actually decrease their cost per item produced because they won't have the excess overhead costs. As a result, during the beginning of an economic recovery, company's profits tend to rise steeply without the need to raise prices.

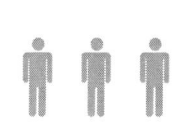

TVMEC AND THE THREE PILLARS OF THE ECONOMY

PILLAR 1: NEW TREASURY BONDS (RELEASING INVESTMENT CAPITAL)

The initial plan is to break the $300 billion printed up into three equal $100 billion sections representing the three pillars of the economy with the understanding that these amounts aren't fixed and can be changed among the educational, infrastructural and working capital pillars in future years as the needs of the economy change or become clearer.

A destructive economic effect of our government's budget deficit is it takes investment dollars away from the capital pillar to finance the debt. This limits economic growth, reduces the taxes the government could have received, and leads to future deficits. TVMEC will release this investment capital to stimulate the economy and minimize future deficits, while paying off the underlying debt at the same time.

The capital pillar will be serviced through the issuance of a new treasury bond to be purchased using the government sector holdings. Although the stated rate of return the government pays on the entire amount of the bonds is still 2 percent, the effective rate of return is 5.7 percent when using TVMEC to provide both a higher rate of return and payoff the underlying debt. This rate is lower than the 6.4 percent from the earlier example because now we're paying off the underlying debt too. There's no reason to keep rolling the debt over into a new bond and keep paying off one credit card with another—the bill will be paid in full.

In order for the time value of money to kick in and the compounding of interest to really take hold for the capital pillar, I developed a one hundred year payback schedule with an initial amount down of $2 billion provided by the government sector's social security fund and interest being compounded semi-annually at a 2 percent rate. The $2 billion amount was tiered down with 100 one-year intervals of $20 million each (a $1.98 billion, ninety-nine year bond, a $1.96 billion ninety-eight year bond, …, a one-year $20 million bond), resulting in a total of $99 billion printed up. This $99 billion printed up to buy these bonds allows the government to pay off other bonds coming due that year and release those funds to the capital pillar.

With the $99 billion printed up added to the initial $2 billion put down, the process starts out with $101 billion in the first year. At a 2 percent interest rate it earns $2.02 billion in interest. TVMEC takes $20 million from the $2.02 billion in interest and uses it to pay off the debt from the one-year $20 million bond at the bottom of the tier. The other $2 billion in interest is used to buy other bonds so at the start of the second year the process now has $103 billion in loans earning 2 percent interest per year. During the second year, $2.06 billion is earned in interest and $40 million is taken from this amount to pay off the debt of the $40 million two-year loan from the tier schedule. The other $2.02 billion in interest left is used to buy more loans. The process continues throughout the 100-year period with the last year paying off the initial $2 billion put down by the social security funds. The bottom line in Figure 2 shows the amount of debt paid off and destroyed per year with the tiered down schedule from the interest payments. The sum of all the individual payments, which would be represented by the area under the line would equal $101 billion—the initial $2 billion invested by the social security fund plus the $99 billion printed up. The top, dashed line represents the extra interest available each year after paying off the bond for the printed money due that year. Notice that by year 100 more than five times as much additional interest is generated than in year 1. This is due to the compounding power of the excess interest from the previous years. The total amount of excess interest over the 100-year period, represented by the area under the dashed line, adds up to $513 billion. For the $2 billion put down by the social security fund, this equates to the equivalent of a 5.7 percent return on their money.

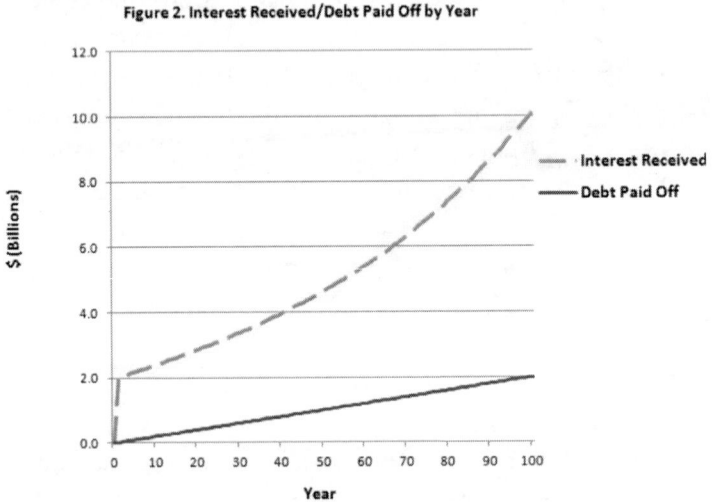

Figure 2. Interest Received/Debt Paid Off by Year

If the same $101 billion amount were to be invested in treasury bills each year for 100 years ($2 billion from social security funds and $99 billion from printed money), the total amount of debt available to be paid off at the one hundred-year point would be over $29.6 trillion. Taking one hundred years to pay off the debt may seem like a long time, but it's necessary to pay back the debt slowly over a long period of time to prevent a glut of investment capital. Failure to do so would lead to another bubble in the stock market like we had at the beginning of the millennium when the market crashed. The one hundred year period certainly suffices for a long time and the impact of the amounts to be paid back at such a distant point in the future will be negligible. Assuming a 3 percent rate of inflation, the impact of taking $2 billion out of the economy one hundred years from now would be equivalent to taking out only $89 million today due to the time value of money.

While the interest from the loans is paying off the national debt, the increase in the money supply is minimizing future deficits. If we assume we'd receive 2/3 of the increased money supply back in new taxes and lose the other 1/3, the increased money supply effects from the new treasury bonds would produce an extra $67 billion in tax revenue during the first year, $133 billion the second year, and $200 billion per year in subsequent years when compared to the current system not using TVMEC (see Figure 3). The net result would be a $19.8 trillion total increase in new revenue over the one hundred year period (see Figure 4). This $19.8 trillion is outside of the interest process which would separately pay off $29.6 trillion in debt during that time. When the effects of the two are combined, we'd be able to pay off or reduce the future debt by $49.4 trillion from the new treasury bonds when compared to our current system.

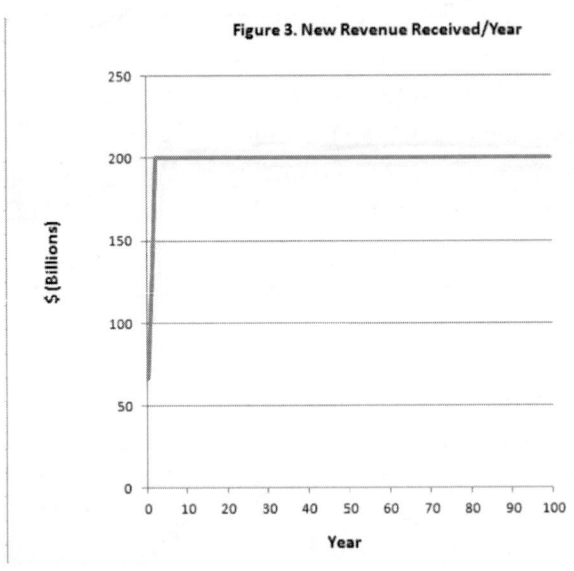

Figure 3. New Revenue Received/Year

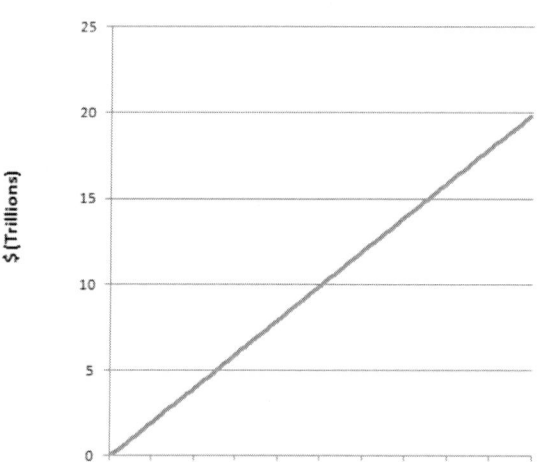

Figure 4. Cumulative New Revenue

That $49.4 trillion figure is actually very conservative. I didn't factor several other benefits into the equation. For instance, once the government sector loans are all covered by the new treasury bonds, the private sector loans could also be converted. Instead of paying around 5 percent interest (as is currently forecast by 2015 under our current system), we would then be paying 2 percent. That 3 percent savings in interest on one hundred billion dollars in loans means we'd be paying

$3 billion less in interest payments the first year, $6 billion less the second, $9 billion less the third, and so on if we continue to loan $100 billion per year in this manner. It also doesn't take into account that after year two we'll be destroying the extra tax income from the printed money to keep the money supply constant, and we'll write off that amount of debt from what is due when the printed money is paid off. When that printed money is paid off in the future, there's no requirement to destroy it anymore, since it was destroyed earlier, so it now becomes extra income (up to $100 billion per year over the life of the loan [maximum potential of $9.8 trillion throughout the cycle when all the money is paid back] depending on how much was lost from the system when taxes were collected. You won't see most of it, however, until the latter years when the majority of the printed money is scheduled to be paid back and destroyed).

PILLAR 2: EDUCATIONAL LOANS (IMPROVING EDUCATION)

What would you say if I told you it was possible for everyone who qualifies to get into college to afford it? Through TVMEC it's possible. A typical $60,000 college loan for a state college would be made available at a 2 percent rate. For the first ten years of the loan, the student would only have to pay the interest. The principal would be paid off during the next ten years. This would allow the new graduate to pay only $1,200 per year for the first ten years without being strapped financially with high student loan payments during the period when they're getting established in their career field. They could afford to work outside their career field and still be able to pay $100 monthly. Even after the ten year interest-only period, the combined principal and interest payments at a 2 percent interest rate would still be only $552 per month. By that time, they should be established in their career field and able to afford their payments.

When I first mentioned this idea to a friend, he told me it's already possible (if you're one of the lucky few to qualify) to get a college loan for as low as 1 percent, so why would they want a 2 percent loan? The answer is the terms of the deal. A ten-year 1 percent loan requires a payment of $525 per month for ten years. My loan would only require a $100 monthly payment for the first ten years. Many college graduates find it hard to obtain a well-paying job in their field of study when they first graduate because they don't have any experience, so they can't afford to pay rent, car payments, and a $525 monthly student loan on their initial salary. The additional $425 monthly discretionary income gained by using the 2 percent loan with payments of only $100 per month during these hard times can be a significant boost to their financial health. Assuming they did have the ability to pay the entire $525 a month though, had they instead chosen the $100 a month option and invested the other $425 in the tax-free treasury bonds at 5 percent, at the ten-year mark when they would have finished making payments on the 1 percent loan, they'd have $65,395 worth of treasury bills accumulated off their $425 monthly investments. When the principle payments are added to the interest payments at the ten-year mark, the new loan payments rise to $552 a month. The student could make these $552 a month payments from their $65, 395 worth of treasury bills and keep the rest invested. When the 2 percent loan is paid off ten years later, they'd still have $23,581 left in treasury bonds. Which loan would you choose?

The above example assumed the federal government would be handling the loans, but with over 1.6 million loans annually this would require additional levels of bureaucracy which would increase the costs. Therefore, the way I'd suggest implementing these loans is by using the banking system as the middleman. The banks would initiate the loans with the students and collect the payments. The government would supply the money through TVMEC. The government would print up the money and off-set the need for issuing new treasury bonds by balancing it against the accounts receivable from the loans. The initial amount printed up for the program would be $100 billion per year, allowing over 1.6 million high school graduates access to the money. In order to qualify for the loan, you only need to be accepted to college—providing incentives for people to stay in school and apply themselves.

The banking industry would probably want their cut, too, but it shouldn't be too big of a cut and should be federally restricted. They normally make their money on loans through the difference between what they have to pay depositors for their money and the rate they charge borrowers for their loans. The spread between the two has to be large enough to cover any defaults, but in this case, it isn't their money at risk—it's the government's money, so they don't need to add to the spread. Since there isn't much room for profits (if any) on a 2 percent loan in the first place (considering the number of defaults), a 1/2 percent fee seems fair. Even if we put a 1/2 percent add-on to the loan to make it worthwhile for the banking industry, the ensuing 2.5 percent rate would only increase the monthly payments by $25 (to $125) during the first ten years and by $14 (to $566) during the next ten. Had the student been able to make the payments for a 1 percent loan but chosen the 2 percent loan instead and invested the difference, he'd still have $14,630 left over after the loan was paid off. The $125 payment would still be affordable and within reach of a recent college graduate. Since the banking industry wouldn't be risking any of their own money, everything they received would be pure profit—adding to their solvency.

The printed money would follow the same schedule and duration as the new treasury bonds did. They'd be printed up with the one hundred year tier schedule, and the printed money would be destroyed according to that schedule. Since the loans are only twenty-year student loans, the two schedules don't exactly match up. As a result, when the principal is being paid off for the twenty-year loans, the principal will exceed what's due to be destroyed according to the one hundred year payback schedule. The excess principal that isn't destroyed according to the one hundred-year payback schedule can be re-loaned to help account for inflation and keep the opportunities to go to college open for as many students as possible, even as the price of college tuition rises. The 2 percent interest collected will also be used in this manner, with an additional $2 billion being available from the previous year's interest payments in year two, $4 billion in interest from the previous 2 year's interest payments in year three, $6 billion the next year, and so on to reduce the impact of rising tuition.

The impact from the education loans on the federal debt would be the same as for the new treasury bonds. The interest payment amounts are the same. The only difference is it's the students who are paying the interest, and they're paying it on student loans instead of the government paying the interest on the treasury bonds. An additional $29.6 trillion could be paid off from a future debt one hundred years from now on top of the $29.6 trillion that could be paid off from the new treasury bonds. Total additional new revenue created during that one hundred year period would be increased by another $19.8 trillion, as well. After the second year, the excess tax revenue would also be destroyed for the printed money on these loans, and the accounts receivable for the loans would be credited for the amount needed to be destroyed in the future. With student loan payments of only $125 a month for the first ten years, the number of defaults should be lower than what it has historically been. However, the 67 percent cushion against defaults created by destroying the excess tax revenue in an effort to minimize inflationary pressures should cover any defaults that do occur.

For those parents who have diligently saved their money for their kid's education, there's a special treat. They can not only keep their money, but get a return on it while using that money to pay off the TVMEC loan. This treat would require a twenty five-year loan with the first ten years being interest only, but it's something for the government to explore. If the parent can receive the equivalent of a 4.85 percent return on the money earmarked for their child's education during the first ten years, the $60,000 would grow to $93,267 at the end of the ten years (assuming the child paid the interest during the period). If they still were able to get a 4.85 percent rate of return over the next fifteen years while the loan was being paid off, they would receive $4,673 a year in interest (before taxes). The price of the loan payment would be $4,670 a year (before tax credits). Not only would their parents save their $60,000, but they'd keep the whole $93,267 it grew into after the loan was paid off. That's the equivalent of a 1.78 percent return on their money over the twenty-five year period, which is a lot better than not having anything. With the government forecasting to be paying a 5 percent interest rate on its tax-free ten-year treasury bills by 2015, this 4.85 percent rate is definitely achievable.

The 2 percent educational loans would also lead to greater social mobility. Instead of a redistribution of wealth through a tax hike on the rich, it would provide a redistribution of opportunity to create wealth. Give a man a fish, and you'll feed him for a day. Teach a man to fish, and you'll feed him for life. Education is the key to improving your social position in life. Providing an additional 1.6 million students with loans annually will give them not only the opportunity to improve their position, but the motivation to study and stay in school, as well. If they know the opportunity is there, it's up to them to decide if they want to take it or not. If they choose not to take the opportunity, it was their choice, and they'll have to live with it. These loans could also be used to re-train people who've lost their jobs with no chance of getting them back due to functional obsolescence. It will provide them with the means needed to start over in a career field they'd enjoy, which should also translate into a lower unemployment rate.

PILLAR 3: INFRASTRUCTURE LOANS (IMPROVING INFRASTRUCTURE)

How does this infrastructure part work? If a state or local government is looking at a long-term project to improve its roads, bridges, build new schools, or add services to a new subdivision being built (such as sewer lines), it may have to issue municipal bonds to pay for it. It first decides the size of the payments it can afford to make and it then issues only enough bonds at the going interest rate that it can afford to pay. Additional construction not immediately required is put off until the next year's budget. By the year 2015, the states will have to offer between 5 and 6 percent to compete with treasury bonds for the investor's money. If instead of paying a rate of 5 to 6 percent on their bonds, the states are able to pay only 2 percent, they could afford to do more construction. The amount of construction it could afford up front while making the same payments for the same amount of time would increase by 30.5 percent compared to a 5 percent rate and by 50.2 percent compared to a 6 percent rate on a twenty five-year bond. I'm using these 5 to 6 percent interest rates for comparison purposes, not so much because it's what we're currently paying, but because it's what our own government is expecting to be paying by the year 2015 and by the end of the decade, as mentioned earlier. If they're eventually paying higher rates, that amount would increase even further. These amounts assume the state has a balanced budget, and they aren't just rolling over the payment of the principal on new municipal bonds, but are actually paying off the debt. If the state is running a budget deficit and actually only paying the interest on the loans while rolling over the principal, the up-front purchasing power is greatly increased. They could afford 106 percent and 162 percent more construction up front, versus the 5 percent or 6 percent rates on their municipal bonds, while making the exact same amounts and still have the same amount of debt after twenty-five years. If instead of performing more construction, these deficit-running states wanted to reduce their costs, they could perform the same amount of construction and the total cost would drop by 51.6 percent compared to a 5 percent rate twenty five-year bond and by 61.8 percent compared to a 6 percent rate twenty five-year bond. This huge drop in financing costs could help them turn their budget deficits into surpluses without raising taxes or cutting services.

Mechanically, the infrastructure loans work pretty much the same way as the educational loans do, only we don't need to use the banks as the middlemen. State and local governments would be able to get their loans directly from the federal government at the 2 percent rate. The impact from the infrastructure loans on the federal debt would be the same as for the new treasury bonds and the education loans. An additional $29.6 trillion could be paid off from a future debt one hundred years from now on top of the $59.2 trillion that could be paid off from the new treasury bonds and educational loans. The total additional new revenue created during that one hundred year period would be increased by another $19.8 trillion, as well. After the second year, the excess tax revenue would also be destroyed for the printed money for these loans, and the accounting for the printed money would be credited appropriately, providing a huge insurance policy against defaults on the infrastructure loans…not that we'd expect the state and local governments to default. When the additional principal above what was due to be destroyed comes in, it would again be available to decrease the current year's federal deficit.

An alternative way of using the infrastructure loans would decrease our dependence on foreign oil, as well as reduce our carbon footprint. After the Great Depression, we put the economy back together by increasing the backbone of America—its roads, waterways, and power plants. In addition to the roads being built or maintained through the infrastructure loans, we can also make the United States more energy efficient through the use of renewable energy.

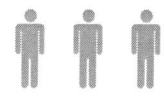

TVMEC VS TAX CUTS

So far, we've discussed the time value of money, shown how it can be used to pay off the national debt while strengthening the three pillars of the economy, and shown how it can be used to prevent future debt. Now I'd like to compare TVMEC to the current system to show why TVMEC should be used instead of tax cuts. I'll start with an explanation of primary dollars, the money multiplier, and buying power, because these three things are common to both systems.

I'll use my own defined concept of primary dollars to visualize what the money multiplier does in terms of buying power. A primary dollar is a dollar at the beginning of the money multiplier cycle. It represents the original dollar spent and affected by the money multiplier. A dollar in the later stages (after the first collection of taxes) is not considered a primary dollar.

The money multiplier is the number of times money is spent in the money supply before it is all absorbed by taxes. The mathematical relationship of the money multiplier to the tax rate is 1/x, where x is the tax rate. If the tax rate is 50 percent (0.50 times your income), the money multiplier would be 1 / 0.50 = 2. If the tax rate is 33 1/3 percent, the money multiplier would be 1 / 0.33 = 3. For an example of how it works, I'll use a 50 percent tax rate. The first time money is spent, 100 percent of the initial amount is spent, and 50 percent would be collected in taxes with the other 50 percent staying in the money supply. When this 50 percent still in the money supply is spent again, half of it would be collected in taxes and the other half (now representing only 25 percent of the original amount) would remain in the money supply. When this 25 percent of the original amount is spent, half would be collected for taxes and the other half (now 12.5 percent of the original amount) would remain in the money supply and so on until nothing is left. The sum of the 100 percent, 50 percent, 25 percent, 12.5 percent, etc. would result in the equivalent of nearly 100 percent of the money being spent a second time for a money multiplier of two. The concept of the money multiplier assumes no outflows or inflows of cash from the economy (such as trade deficits/surpluses or balances on current accounts). Although outflows and inflows of cash exist in the real world, the money multiplier is still a useful tool for calculating the effects of changes on the economy.

Buying power is the number of primary dollars times the money multiplier. This represents the value of goods and services that could be bought (without deficit spending) with the money in the money supply before it is all taken back in through taxes. On the demand side of the law of supply and demand, changes in buying power lead to changes in demand and therefore to changes in the prices of goods (on the supply side, changes in the costs of producing the goods lead to changes in the prices of goods).

Putting aside the fact TVMEC would be paying off the deficit while tax cuts would not, I'd like to explain the differences between tax cuts and TVMEC through the use of two examples and buying power. The examples won't use the $300 billion/year TVMEC I'm advocating for, just a made-up amount for comparison purposes between using tax cuts and TVMEC.

With a tax cut, the money supply stays constant. The number of times the money can be used before being absorbed by taxes (the money multiplier) increases. The result is an increase in buying power, the number of goods being purchased, and the GDP of the economy. If the tax rate is 25 percent (20 percent federal and 5 percent state taxes) and the number of primary dollars is $3.5 trillion, the money multiplier of four would put the buying power at $14 trillion. If the federal tax rate was cut by 1 percent to 19 percent, the new tax rate would be 24 percent (19 percent federal + 5 percent state), the new money multiplier would be 4.17, and the new buying power would be $14.583 trillion. The government would potentially still be able to receive the same $3.5 trillion in taxes (although the state government would now be receiving a higher percentage of it). During the second year the tax cut is in effect, the number of primary dollars would still be constant at $3.5 trillion, and the money multiplier would be 4.17 again (because the tax rates would be the same as during the first year). The buying power would remain the same at $14.583 trillion. Although the people are still enjoying a tax break relative to what it would have been if a tax cut hadn't been enacted, this tax break is creating no new economic buying power beyond the first year of the tax cut. Therefore, any new economic growth stimulated by the tax cut actually takes place in the first year, alone. The economy is then dependent on the tax cut remaining in effect indefinitely for any benefits to last. If the tax cut was temporary, at the future date when the tax cut ended, the money multiplier would decline again back to its original amount, and the buying power would decline to its original amount, as well, potentially resulting in an economic recession. What are the benefits of using a tax cut then? The stimulated economy can support employing more people. Each percentage in the unemployment rate equates to $50 billion in government expenditures/losses of revenue.[20] If the tax cut enables the unemployment rate to decrease by 3 percent (during periods of high unemployment), the government would be saving $150 billion a year relative to what it would have been spending. One warning about using tax cuts though is the government has no control over what the tax cuts are spent on and where the money goes. As a result, the money might not lead to economic development. For instance, if I receive a tax cut of $600, and I invest it all in buying treasury bonds, no increase in economic growth would result from this investment. The government would just be receiving $600 less in tax revenues, have $600 more in debt, and would now be paying interest on that increased $600 in debt. Similarly, if I take the $600 tax break and go on vacation to Panama where the US dollar is the primary currency, the dollar enters the Panamanian economy and stays there. The government has again incurred additional debt without gaining any economic benefit.

Under TVMEC, the money multiplier stays constant, but the number of primary dollars is increased.

If the tax rate is 25 percent, and the money supply is $3.5 trillion, the money multiplier of four would still put the buying power at $14 trillion. If $145.75 billion were printed up, the number of primary dollars would increase to $3.65 trillion, and the new buying power would be $14.583 trillion. The government potentially recovers up to $3.65 trillion in taxes. Although the inflationary pressures of the increased buying power were the same for both cases, the government was able to receive an additional $145 billion in taxes by using TVMEC, versus tax cuts. The reduction in unemployment benefits would also be the same as it would have been for using tax cuts. During the second year of TVMEC, the additional $145.75 billion printed up results in increases in both the buying power and in inflationary pressures associated with it to 15.166 trillion. The increased buying power would also be accompanied by a further increase in tax revenue to $291.5 billion more than would have been available without using TVMEC. Although the TVMEC program would increase tax revenue and decrease unemployment, it appears it would also lead to higher inflation.

Through these two examples, we've learned tax cuts produce an economic stimulus and reduce unemployment, but the economic benefits are primarily received only in the first year of the program (with the exception of lower unemployment, throughout). We've also learned TVMEC would be able to create the same amount of economic stimulus, more tax revenues would be received, unemployment would decrease, and these effects could be compounded in future years—but only at the risk of increased inflation (or so it would seem).

Although increased inflation may seem like a deficiency inherent in the TVMEC process, I've found a way to turn it off. I've found a way to use TVMEC to fine-tune governmental income to help prevent annual deficits while decreasing inflationary pressures through a trade-off system of transfers. We haven't mentioned the other factor TVMEC has that tax cuts don't have— a debt of printed money to be paid back and destroyed. Suppose (in the example above) a decision was made to increase the buying power to $15.166 trillion (as well as tax revenues by $291.5 billion/year to prevent further annual deficits) and keep it there. I've already shown TVMEC can get it there while increasing tax revenue by $145.75 billion per year for two consecutive years, but how do we keep it there? The answer is to predict the increase in the money supply for the next year and destroy it when it is received back in new taxes. Since we'd be destroying the amount of money we print up that stayed in the system, the net effect would be no change in discretionary income. We'd still be receiving

$291.5 billion a year more in taxes than we would have otherwise, but the money supply would be stable, and the buying power would be constant at $15.166 trillion.

TVMEC shouldn't be used to chase budget deficits. Instead of capping the money supply at a level that makes sense for the overall economy, unscrupulous politicians could continue to let it increase until the amount of money received in new tax revenue will balance the budget for them. At that point, they could increase their spending and allow TVMEC to increase the money supply again to cover their new level of spending. This would lead to disaster in the end, and TVMEC would take the blame instead of the unscrupulous politicians. The amount of money released under TVMEC into the money supply should always be a low percentage of the total money supply, or else the value of the dollar in the international market would drop. This is why I advocate for the Federal Reserve Board to be in charge of how much should be printed up each year based on the state of the economy instead of letting Congress make that decision. TVMEC could be another tool in the economic tool shed that could work alongside the discount rate and reserve requirements.

If we want to use TVMEC to balance the budget, it can be done, but it will take time. As discussed earlier, the normal business cycle includes periods of recession.

It is only during the times of recessions that TVMEC should be used to expand the money supply without destroying the excess money received in taxes. In doing so, the tax base and tax revenues will be increased, and, eventually after several cycles, the budget will be balanced. That doesn't forego the need for the government to attempt to balance its books in the meantime, or TVMEC will be chasing an ever-changing figure.

Another thing I'd like to emphasize is TVMEC can be turned on or turned off at any time. The TVMEC system is not dependent on itself for survival. The economic effects and amount of debt paid off by the policy for one year will continue regardless if TVMEC is used again in subsequent years. Since the payback is heavily weighted toward the end of the time stream and since the impact of taking the money out at the future date is extremely reduced due to the effects of inflation on the time value of money, stopping at any point would have minimal impact compared to the gains received. Paying off the entire debt using TVMEC will take many years. If a better system comes along, TVMEC can be discontinued, and the economy would still be better off than if it hadn't been used.

Another item I'd like to point out is that the inflationary impact from the TVMEC system would only take place in the first three years. The stabilization of the money supply through paying back printed money with the expected tax revenue increase for the year would keep the number of primary dollars constant and eliminate inflationary pressures from the fourth year on.

ORGANIZATION

It would seem ideal to have TVMEC fall under the Department of the Treasury, so payments could be closely monitored and those who didn't keep up with their payments could easily be tracked down at year's end when they file for their taxes. However, TVMEC institutionally aligns itself more along the lines of what the Federal Reserve System does than what the Department of the Treasury does. According to the Federal Reserve Board website,

> The Federal Reserve System was chartered in 1913 to provide the nation with a safer, more flexible, and more stable monetary and financial system. Over the years, its roles have evolved and expanded. Today, the Federal Reserve's duties include conducting the nation's monetary policy by influencing money and credit conditions in the economy in pursuit of full employment and stable prices; promoting the stability of the financial system; providing banking services to depository institutions and

to the federal government; and ensuring that consumers receive adequate information and fair treatment in their interactions with the banking system.[21]

Since TVMEC's implementation will have a direct affect on the nation's monetary policy, credit conditions, rate of employment, rate of inflation, and stability of the financial system, making the Federal Reserve System also be responsible for the implementation of TVMEC only makes sense. The charter for the Federal Reserve System is also more in line with what TVMEC needs for successful implementation, too. It says:

> The Federal Reserve System is not "owned" by anyone and is not a private, profit-making institution. Instead, it is an independent entity within the government, having both public purposes and private aspects…
>
> As the nation's central bank, the Federal Reserve derives its authority from the U.S. Congress. It is considered an *independent* central bank because its decisions do not have to be ratified by the President or anyone else in the executive or legislative branch of government, it does not receive funding appropriated by the Congress, and the terms of the members of the

> Board of Governors span multiple presidential and congressional terms. However, the Federal Reserve *is* subject to oversight by the Congress, which periodically reviews its activities and can alter its responsibilities by statute. Also, the Federal Reserve must work within the framework of the overall objectives of economic and financial policy established by the government. Therefore, the Federal Reserve can be more accurately described as "independent within the government".[22]

The Federal Reserve Board is responsible to Congress, which already has the ability to alter the board's responsibilities, so implementation of TVMEC can easily be added. Its decisions don't have to be ratified by the President, and its Board of Governor's terms span multiple presidential and congressional terms, so politics can be taken out of the game, and the focus can remain on the long term implementation and impact of TVMEC. Since the Federal Reserve must work within the framework of the overall objectives of economic and financial policy established by the government, it must anticipate the government's revenue needs and can adjust the amount of money printed up and/or paid back and destroyed to help the government reach its goals while minimizing inflationary pressures.

The Federal Reserve System, although a non-profit organization, is already providing a surplus to the government, which is paid directly to the US Treasury. According to the Federal Reserve Board's 2010 annual report, the payment was $79.2 billion in 2010. Its income is derived primarily from the interest on the Reserve Banks' holdings of US government securities and from fees they charge depository institutions for providing services (such as processing and clearing checks).[23] Since the Federal Reserve is already dealing closely with the US government securities, wouldn't it only be natural to let them be responsible for overseeing the TVMEC process to pay off these securities? Since they process and clear all the checks in the system and already have contacts with all the banks and financial institutions, wouldn't it also be natural for them to act like a general contractor to member banks and be the clearing house for the student and government loans? With technological changes and improvements in the banking system over the past two decades, students could be required to sign up for automatic fund transfers from their banking accounts when they're approved for the student loans. It would be automatic for them—just like paying rent—and it would have to be done, making it so they couldn't blow their money in other areas without first paying their loans.

How would TVMEC fit in with the Federal Reserve's monetary policy? The Federal Reserve currently conducts monetary policy using three major tools: [24]

> (1) Open market operations—the buying and selling of US Treasury and federal agency securities in the open market.
>
> (2) Discount rate—the interest rate charged depository institutions on loans from their Federal Reserve Bank's lending facility (the discount window).
>
> (3) Reserve requirements—requirements regarding the amount of funds that depository institutions must hold in reserve against deposits made by their customers.
>
> Using these tools, the Federal Reserve influences the demand for and supply of balances that depository institutions hold on deposit at Federal Reserve Banks (the key component of reserves), and thus the federal funds rate—the rate at which depository institutions trade balances at the Federal Reserve. Changes in the federal funds rate trigger a chain of events that

> affect other short-term interest rates, foreign exchange rates, long-term interest rates, the amount of money and credit, and, ultimately, a range of economic variables, including employment, output, and prices of goods and services.

In other words, the Federal Reserve buys and sells securities to control the amount of money in the money supply. When the money supply is low, the Federal Reserve buys securities and frees up money for the individual and institutional investors. It uses the discount rate and reserve requirements to influence how much money banks have available to lend and how much it costs to lend money. TVMEC will give the Federal Reserve a fourth tool for controlling the money supply. Like the first tool, it will directly influence the amount of securities bought and sold, and, therefore, the money supply. TVMEC will expand the money supply through loans. TVMEC can constrict the money supply by paying back and destroying the printed up money, or by halting the loaning out of money during a year while still receiving and destroying the principal from loans made in previous years. As you can see, the Federal Reserve System is already statutorily set up as being the perfect place for the implementation of TVMEC, and it only increases their flexibility in controlling the nation's monetary policies.

TVMEC can be used in conjunction with the Federal Reserve's current policy to fill in the gaps. These gaps can be seen in an excerpt of the non-partisan Concord Coalition's "Report on Fiscal Responsibility" for July 2003. According to their website, the Concord Coalition is "a non-partisan, grassroots organization dedicated to educating the public about the causes and consequences of federal budget deficits, the long-term challenges facing America's unsustainable entitlement programs, and how to build a sound foundation for economic growth. Their report states:

> The first six months of the 108th Congress were the most fiscally irresponsible in recent memory. The crux of the problem was a schizophrenic pursuit of small government tax policies and big government spending initiatives. Following the lead of the Bush Administration, Congress made no attempt to reconcile the cost of new tax cuts and spending initiatives within the framework of a realistic long-term balanced budget plan. Instead, policymakers took a deteriorating budget outlook and made it worse…

Adding insult to injury, Congress used deceptive accounting gimmicks that would land a corporate CEO in jail. It is hard to say which is worse—the "sunset" gimmick used to hide the cost of an unaffordable tax cut, the "doughnut hole" gimmick used to hide the cost of an unaffordable, new Medicare entitlement, the shell games used to hide the likely cost of appropriations, or the disingenuous budget resolution that lead to such shenanigans in the first place.[25]...

The actual revenue loss [due to the tax cuts] will be much higher than the official $350 billion estimate. To keep the official estimate within a limit agreed to in the Senate, the legislation assumed that the new tax breaks will expire, or "sunset" within five years. No one even pretended that this was a realistic assumption. It was pure gimmickry. Senator Olympia Snowe (R-ME) had it right when she said, 'This is a one trillion dollar tax cut masquerading as $350 billion.'"

The 108th Congress implemented President Bush's tax cuts without coming up with a way of offsetting the revenue shortfall. On paper, they claimed the tax cuts were temporary and they'd be allowed to expire (called sunsetting), resulting in only a $350 billion loss in revenue. In reality, they knew it wouldn't sunset and the true cost would be much higher in terms of lost revenue. Eight years has passed since this report was written and the tax cuts still haven't sunsetted. At the same time they were reducing tax revenue, they were increasing Medicare benefits with no way to pay for these benefits.

This was only the tip of the iceberg in the sunset game. According the report, of the three tax cuts, which officially sunset between 2004-2020, the official revenue loss is $1.3 trillion; however, none of the tax cuts are realistically expected to actually sunset, so the actual expected revenue loss is three trillion dollars. Why won't they be allowed to sunset? Once the benefits of a tax cut are enacted, the tax cuts must stay in effect for the same level of buying power to remain. If not, the money multiplier would revert to its previous level, and the buying power would be reduced. If the tax cuts are allowed to sunset, the resulting reduction in buying power would slow down the economy. The tax cuts could be allowed to sunset without adverse economic results if it were accompanied by an additional increase in buying power at the same time. This is where TVMEC could come in as a useful tool. As the tax cuts are allowed to sunset, TVMEC could restore the lost buying power by increasing the number of primary dollars—thus canceling the adverse effects of the sunset.

When the report mentions the doughnut hole gimmick, it's referring to gaps between the Medicare plans' front-end coverage and catastrophic backstop. The report refers to arbitrary holes in coverage which could cost from $60 billion to $200 billion to cover and states "the simple truth, however, is that Medicare's existing benefit package is unaffordable. Congress shouldn't add new benefits until it ensures that we can afford the ones we already have."[26] Once again, TVMEC can come to the rescue. As shown earlier, TVMEC can easily increase tax revenues by at least $200 billion a year, which would fill in the doughnut hole.

With the "shell games used to hide the costs of appropriations," the report was talking about the expiration of the "pay go" law and how Congress found a loop-hole by using an exemption to hide the additional $1.7 trillion in tax cuts when it doesn't sunset. Once again, TVMEC could allow the sunset to happen, so the impact wouldn't be the loss of $1.7 trillion in tax revenue. TVMEC would increase the money supply which would provide the stimulus needed to counteract the reduction in economic activity caused by the increased tax rate. With President Obama talking about letting the Bush tax cuts sunset, we need a backup plan to fill in the monetary gap and keep the economy from retracting and TVMEC should be seriously considered for that role.

As you can tell, TVMEC could be a powerful tool for the Federal Reserve Board to get us back on track financially and to solve the shortcomings of the current system. When used in conjunction with the other tools, it will provide them with the flexibility they need to accomplish their responsibilities.

TVMEC USE IN FOREIGN POLICY

TVMEC can also be used to help out our allies or to rebuild countries after wars—at little to no cost to the United States. For instance, take one of our strongest allies in the war on drugs; Colombia. According to the CIA World Fact Book, Colombia has a GDP of $171.6 billion, an inflation rate of 5.5 percent, and a Gross Public Debt that's 52.8 percent of their GDP, yet they still nearly balance their budget with revenues of $63.69 billion and expenditures of $64.96 billion.[27] With an inflation rate of 5.5 percent, they must be paying at least that rate on their debt, or investors would be losing purchasing power. The 52.8 percent of $171.6 billion equates to just over $90.6 billion in debt. Even at a 5.5 percent rate, their debt payments would be around $5 billion a year (nearly 8 percent of their total budget). Now, suppose we use TVMEC to print up $90.6 billion to refinance their debt at a 0 percent rate for twenty-five years; their payments would be $3.624

billion per year, and their entire loan would be paid off in the end. The reduction in payment of their debt would drop their expenditures to $63.58 billion, giving them an actual surplus while they're paying off their debt. Although, there would be a small initial drop in the value of the US currency associated with this dilution. Each year as Colombia paid off its debt, we'd be destroying it and returning the number of dollars in circulation back to their normal pre-loan state. At the end of the twenty-five year period, everything would be back to normal for us, but our ally would be debt free, and the people of this South American country would remember how they got there.

TVMEC can also be used to minimize our economic risk during reconstruction in problematic countries like Afghanistan and Iraq. We can tell the foreign governments to determine how much money they need and to print it up themselves. We'll guarantee to keep the value of their currency stable on the international market by using our own TVMEC-printed money to buy up the excess currency. We can hold their currency against the printed money, so we won't need to issue new treasury bonds. Their governments will gain legitimacy and earn credit for the projects they undertake. They'll also be the ones responsible for any poor decisions. Instead of the US having to donate money with nothing to show for it, we'll have their currency as collateral and we can use it to buy their goods and natural resources. This will promote commerce between our nations while helping them to rebuild.

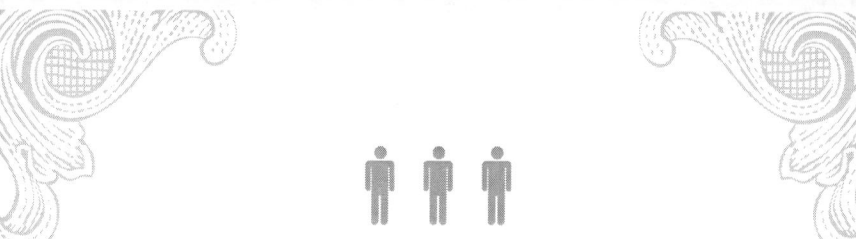

FIXING FORECLOSURE LOANS

One of the major causes of our latest recession was the spiraling drop in house prices, and the accompanying foreclosures that kept the prices dropping. The government's response to help the people keep their homes has been marginal, at best. The government seemed more interested in helping the banks (who were strong-armed by the government into making the poor quality loans in the first place), than it did in helping its constituents. Why? Because the government was afraid the banks would become insolvent if they didn't step in and help them out, and more people would be affected. They didn't look at the big picture to figure out the causes for the high foreclosure rate and think outside of the box to find a solution.

The primary cause of the foreclosure loans was the homeowners had 5-6 percent interest-only loans that could only be for up to 80 percent of the value of the home. As long as home prices were rising, everyone was happy, but when the prices on the homes started dropping below the original cost, the homeowners now had to come up with additional money to keep their loans under the 80 percent mark.

Imagine it's still 2006 and the housing market is still booming. You're a college graduate who just got married and wanted to buy a new home. You're barely making ends meet while renting. You hear stories about people buying houses and then flipping the houses for a profit, while making payments that are less than you pay in rent. You go into a bank to see if you could afford a home and you're told you'd qualify for an interest only loan at a five percent rate, if you can put 20 percent down. Both you and your wife call your parents and beg them for help raising the money. You point to the easy profits being made by people flipping houses, the consistently rising prices of houses and let them know that after you have children and outgrow your starter house, you'll sell it and pay back them back with the profits. Your parents agree and between them they come up with the down payment. At the signing for the loan, the banker mentions the loan can be for only 80 percent of the value of the house and if the value of the house drops, you'll have to come up with the difference, but that shouldn't be an issue since houses generally appreciate in value, not depreciate over time. You buy your starter house for $100,000 with an $80,000 loan from the bank and $20,000 from your parents.

Now fast forward to 2011. You receive a notice from the bank stating your house is now valued at only $75,000. Under the loan agreement, your loan can only be for 80 percent of the value of your house, so the maximum amount your loan can be for has dropped to $60,000. The bank is worried the value of your house will drop further and you'll walk away from the loan like other people have, so they want the other $20,000 to protect their equity in the home. Since you've made all your payments on time, they're willing to give you three months to come up with the additional funds. You've now got 3 children and you've outgrown this starter house, but you have no equity in it; so you can't afford to sell it to move into a bigger house. In fact, since your house is only worth $75,000 and you still owe $80,000 on it, your house is not an asset to you; it's a $5,000 liability. If you let the house go into foreclosure, it'll ruin your credit and you won't be able to buy another house anyways. It would even be hard to find a house to rent, because when the owners of the rental house do a background check on you, the foreclosure will come up and you'll look like a high risk candidate. It doesn't matter that you always made your payments on time, because they'll assume you were fiscally irresponsible. Your parents say it makes no sense to throw good money after bad, since the value of your house is expected to drop further before the housing market recovers, so they won't loan you any more money. Looks like your house will be going into foreclosure and you'll all be moving in with your parents for a couple of years. You're not stupid—you have a college degree. You did nothing wrong. You made all your payments on time. There should be another way out of this situation.

As long as the people were able to make their original 5-6 percent interest–only payments, the government could have printed the money and bought the loans from the banks for a period of ten years. During that time, the homeowners continue to make their 5 percent payments without coming up with the additional money. The government would use 3 of the 5 percent payments toward paying off the principal on the loan and keep the other 2 percent. They'd destroy the principal payments, returning the money supply back to normal. After paying off 3 percent of the loan's principle each year for ten years, the individual would have paid off 30 percent of the loan. In the example above, this would amount to $24,000 of the $80,000 loan being paid off after 10 years. The government during that time would have pocketed 20 percent of the loan's value for implementing this program. In this case, the government would have pocketed $16,000 while helping the young couple keep their house. At the end of the ten years, the government would then sell the other 70 percent ($56,000 in the example above) of the loan back to the bank. The value of the loan would be under what it needed to be to qualify under the original terms ($56,000 versus $60,000 maximum value). The bank wouldn't need to foreclose on the house and sell it at a quick sale for less than what was owed on the loan, so it wouldn't lose any money. The cash it received up front from the government would have ended the credit crunch while providing the bank with the solvency it needed without keeping bad loans on its books. The individual homeowner would have 30 percent more equity in his house which he wouldn't have had under the original loan otherwise, and his payments would also now drop by 30 percent since the loan sold back to the bank was for only 70 percent of the original amount. If that's not an incentive not to walk away, I don't know what is. It's a win-win-win situation all around. This same process could also be used to make housing affordable for low-income or first-time homeowners. Making these loans available to them would also quickly enable the housing market to recover and prevent further foreclosures.

SAVING SOCIAL SECURITY

The premise of the Social Security system is people would pay money into the system up front as a forced savings program. Their employers would also contribute to the employee's account by paying into the Social Security system for them too. That money would be invested and when they reached a certain age, they'd be given back a fixed amount of money each month until they passed away (with the amount based on how long an average person would live past the age when the payments to the individual started). The invested money was supposed to provide for a return greater than the rate of inflation so the individual wouldn't lose any purchasing power. The amount they were supposed to receive back was supposed to be fixed and determined by the future value of what they'd paid in. With a stable or growing population, the amount taken in each year should have been more than what was paid out. That hasn't been the case. Our government has decided to treat our Social Security payments as additional tax revenue and invested all our Social Security funds into treasury bonds to fund their excessive spending. In order to keep the debt payments down, they decided not to pay the going market rates for these treasury bonds, but to pay only a 2 percent rate (which is less than the historical 3 percent rate of inflation). This move alone would mean the people who paid into Social Security wouldn't be able to receive the amount of purchasing power they had paid into it on their behalf in the first place.

Unfortunately, the government has also decided to play politics with the Social Security funds. Instead of paying out the fixed amount, which was sustainable by the amount paid in, they've increased the payment amounts to curry favor with elderly voters. As mentioned earlier, in 2010, the government had to pay out $37 billion more than it took in for Social Security. What is the government's solution? Hide the fact they've mismanaged and underpaid Social Security for their own political gains and blame the problem on people living longer than they'd expected, thereby giving them an excuse to push back the age when the people can start receiving Social Security? While there is a thread of truth in people living longer than they did when social security was first started over a half century ago, if they'd invested the money wisely and had been able to obtain a rate of return greater than the rate of inflation, the government wouldn't be in this mess. Luckily for us taxpayers, there is another solution.

As a reminder, the government has already spent the underlying funds for social security, and it only pays a 2 percent rate on these funds, so it can lower the overall effective rate it pays on its loans. Since Social Security is no longer producing a surplus of funds and now the government needs to borrow the difference, its effective loan rate will rise, and its credit rating could be threatened causing the interest rate it has to pay to rise even higher. The government needs a source of 2 percent interest rate funds while Social Security, on the other hand, needs a rate of return greater than the historic 3 percent rate of inflation to have any chance of remaining viable. Three people currently pay into Social Security for each person receiving payments from it, but that's expected to change as the baby boom generation retires. TVMEC can be used to change the ratio so a single person paying in would be able to support 1.6 people receiving. This would allow benefits to expand in a fiscally sound manner. It will also pay off the underlying debt and put the cash back into social security. It does this by increasing the effective rate of return received to 5.7 percent without increasing the amount of interest the government pays above the current 2 percent rate.

Social Security was my original target when I came up with the idea for TVMEC. I used the concept of one hundred years for the term of the loan with the government retaining only 1 percent of the original amount each year and giving the rest back to be invested as mentioned in the capital pillar section. I knew the money Social Security needed and had saved was already tied up in treasury bonds, so I decided to look for a way to release that money. Printing up the money and using it to replace the Social Security funds tied up in treasury bonds was the initial stimulus for the tiered down system. Originally I was looking at using investors with ten-year treasury bonds providing a greater rate of return as the source of funds, but as I started realizing the power of compounding interest and the need for Social Security to obtain a rate greater than the rate of inflation. I started looking at what would happen if I used longer term bonds which no individual investor would be willing to tie his money up in. While calculating the overall rate of return for a one hundred year period, I noticed the amount of revenue produced was over thirty-five times greater than what was produced using our current 2 percent rate of return. Originally, I mistook this to mean the amount of money produced by one person's payments over his lifetime would be thirty-five times greater than under the current system. Then I realized nobody would be paying into social security for one hundred years. Instead, I needed to calculate the payments for the periods during which the person would be receiving payments, so I averaged the payments from years thirty-four to fifty-two and compared these averages to what the payments would be under our current system with the government paying a 2 percent rate. The results were 4.8 times higher. Since the system is currently fiscally sound with a 3:1 ratio of people paying for each person receiving, I divided the 4.8 figure by three to determine how many people a single person's payments would be able to support. The resulting 1.6 number means for each five people paying in, eight people could be receiving payments under the new system without changing benefit levels or the age at which people started receiving payments. Social Security would no longer be a ponzi scheme and the value of what each person took out of Social Security would be greater than the value of what they'd paid in because the effective rate was higher than the historical rate of inflation.

Here's an example of how it works. Assume you paid the government $100 in Social Security taxes. The government would take that $100 and invest it in a $100 one hundred year treasury bond. It would then print up $99 and invest that in a ninety nine year treasury bond and so on down to a $1 one-year treasury note. The original $100 investment would be covering a total of $5,050 worth of debt during the first year. Even at a 2 percent rate, the interest payment received would be $101, providing the $1 needed to pay off the debt printed for the first year, plus an additional $100 in interest. The now $5,150 worth of bonds covered during the second year would receive $103 in interest, paying off the two dollars printed for that year, plus an additional $101. As you can tell, not only will all $5,050 worth of initial debt be paid off by the one hundred year mark, but there will be lots of extra money left over. In fact, there will be $25,662 left over after paying off the $5,050 of initial debt, which equates to a 5.7 percent annual rate of return on the initial $100 worth of Social Security payments put down.

At a time when the Social Security taxes don't even cover the Social Security payments, this process will provide the money needed to cover the gap while providing a rate of return that significantly exceeds the historic rate of inflation. At the same time, all the money printed up to cover the gap will be destroyed through the process and the underlying debt will be paid off. Leveraging the Social Security taxes in a manner which covers over fifty times more debt than the amount coming in will also allow more of the private sector held debt to be covered by these 2 percent loans, thereby further reducing the effective rate paid on our nation's debt and freeing up more money for other areas of the budget. Compare that to the Washington Post's February 17, 2011, article on Obama's budget plan, where Obama is forecasting interest rates to rise to 5 percent by 2015 and 5.3 percent by the end of the decade. By 2017, Obama is predicting the interest payments to be $627 billion that year. If he's using a 5 percent rate to calculate that $627 billion figure, reducing the effective rate to 2.5 percent through these leveraged loans would save over three hundred billion dollars per year just in interest costs alone over his current system.

PREVENTING THE MELTDOWN

The White House is predicting the federal government will be offering ten year US treasury bonds at a 5 percent rate by the year 2015 and the rates are forecast to climb even higher by the end of the decade.[28] US banks have recently been offering loans around 4 percent for thirty year loans and 3.5 percent for fifteen year loans. These loans come from money deposited by customers with the underlying assumption the bank will always have enough money deposited in it to cover the amount of the loans. To make sure this assumption stays true, the bank has to offer a competitive interest rate to keep the depositor's money in their bank. Since the interest paid to depositors by the bank is taxed, by 2015 the banks will have to offer more than a 5 percent rate to stay competitive with the US treasury bonds; even though they'll be receiving less than 5 percent over the next fifteen to thirty years on the loans and losing money. If the government doesn't step in to help, there will be a meltdown of the US banking system. Since the depositor's money is insured by the FDIC, the government would be forced to bailout the banks. This would require multiple bailouts over the next three decades and, with the federal government's current fiscal problems, I doubt it would be able to afford it. As an alternative to more bailouts, I've come up with another TVMEC plan modeled after the foreclosure loan solution.

I first started by comparing the payments for a thirty year 4 percent interest rate loan to the plan I'd used for the TVMEC foreclosure loans where 3 percent of the loan amount went toward paying down the principal and the other 2 percent went to the government. The idea is for the government to provide the loans directly to the homeowners through Fannie Mae or Freddie Mac. For the current thirty year loan at a 4 percent rate, the payments are $477.41 per month on a $100,000 loan and after ten years the homeowner still owes $78,785. For the TVMEC loans, the payments are $416.67 per month and after ten years the homeowner owes $70,000. Over this ten year period, the homeowner would have paid off $8,785 more debt using the TVMEC loan, providing them with an incentive to switch to the new loan. At the same time, they would have paid $7,289 less in monthly payments over the ten year period. Between the increased equity in the house and the savings in monthly payments, the homeowner would be $16,074 better off taking the TVMEC loan. At the same time, the government would have earned $20,000 in new revenue from this $100,000 loan. The $7,289 reduction in payments is the equivalent of a tax rebate of roughly $729 per year, because it represents an increase in after-tax disposable income. This increase in disposable income is just what we need to pull out of our recession and since it doesn't come at the expense of raising taxes (but instead generates new revenue of $2,000/yr per $100,000 worth of loan), it's also a fiscally sound way to generate it.

Although this sounds good on paper at $100,000 per loan, the capital pillar's allotment of $100 billion would only be able to finance one million loans per year. This would also be taking the capital pillar's allotment away from the Social Security solution. As a result, implementing these loans on a scale large enough to affect the fiscal soundness of the banking system would require an increase of the money supply so big it would have a debilitating impact on the value of the US dollar and hyperinflation would be a problem. That doesn't mean we should just reject the concept because it does have merit in helping rebuild the middle class and bringing the lower class out of poverty while providing additional revenue streams for the federal government. Politically, it may even be more desirable during an election year than fixing Social Security, because Social Security still has a few years before the full impact of the problem is felt. It also takes the printed money back out of circulation within ten years which is faster than the one hundred years it takes for Social Security to take all the money back out, so the devaluation of the dollar recovers faster. As such, it may be a viable alternative to using TVMEC to free up money for the capital sector, but then we'd need to address Social Security later. If the Federal Reserve Board deems it sound enough to expand the money supply by more than $300 billion per year (and immediately destroy all excess tax revenues without letting the money supply expand further), this would be a worthy area to put the additional money and we could do both.

Although the loans would be desirable to those who could get them, the real solution to preventing the meltdown in the banking system lies in keeping the interest rates on the ten year US treasury bonds from rising to the 5 percent rate in the first place. By printing up the money for the Social Security system solution and using that money to buy US treasury bonds at the 2 percent rate, we reduce the supply of dollars needed to be raised through the sale of those bonds to the public sector and keep the interest rates low. If the treasury bond rates don't rise to 5 percent, the banks don't have to raise their interest rates. The solution to the social security problem would actually lower the treasury bond rates and prevent this problem from happening.

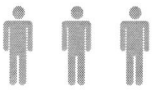

PARTING THOUGHTS

The current state of the economy may not seem strong, but that doesn't mean we can't turn it back around. We never really did get an economic boom after the first market crash this century, although we did have a short-lived bubble in the housing market that quickly popped. The reason is, our economy is not exporting enough while, at the same time, we're relying on everyone else to produce our goods for us as we have "record after record" trade deficits. The value of the dollar is still too high, and it's being kept there by the countries that are relying on these exports to sustain their own growth. Instead of letting the market corrections run their course, trade deficits are being reinvested in our federal debt instead of in our goods, causing the government to run further deficits to prevent a recession. A "Buy American" campaign to get Americans to spend less on foreign goods runs the risk of backfiring because the foreigners own over 44 percent of our publicly held debt, and if they decide to pull it out of our economy, we don't have enough available cash domestically to cover the debt without running the economy dry. Without it, our government would be bankrupt. I'm advocating using TVMEC which would provide over $600 billion per year in new tax revenue within three years without raising the tax rate.

The recent events with major cities like New York, Philadelphia, and Atlanta asking for a piece of the $700 billion bailout loans, and with states like California, tens of billions of dollars in debt show there's a market for TVMEC loans. Student loans would not only provide new opportunities to those who otherwise couldn't afford it, but it would also provide risk-free profits for the banking community; helping the banks to recover without additional bailouts of taxpayer dollars. If companies like GM and Chrysler come up with a survivability plan that would return them to profitability, wouldn't it also make more sense to provide the money in TVMEC loans, rather than to run up our deficit and have to issue new debt to cover those loans? TVMEC also frees us from the economic slavery cycle we're currently headed toward when foreign investors are reinvesting our trade deficits back into our debt payments, causing us to issue new debt to stay out of a recession because TVMEC buys up the loans instead, forcing them to invest in our economy or buy our goods.

Those who are currently manipulating the normal market system by investing their trade surpluses in the United State's debt in order to sustain growth in their own economy should beware. Even though they may be experiencing a long period of growth now, it will be accompanied by a long period of stagnation later. When TVMEC starts releasing their funds from our federal debt, they will be faced with two choices: use their money to buy our goods and services, or invest it in our markets. They won't be able to continue investing in our debts. If they invest it in our markets, our companies will become stronger, and the United State's economy will become more efficient and grow. If they invest in our goods, the trade deficit will become a trade surplus, and once again our companies will have the cash they need to become more efficient and strive—only, it will be through their profits. Either way, our economy will experience an extended period of growth, and the government will no longer need to use deficit spending to prevent a recession. In essence, their investments in our federal debt have become bank deposits for our future growth that will be realized as soon as we start paying off the federal debt.

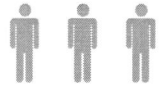

REFERENCES

1 Pride-Ferrell, *Marketing*, Page 35.
2 Ibid, Page 63.
3 Ibid, Page 63.
4 http://www.treasuredirect.gov/NP/BPDLogin?application=np
5 ftp://ftp.publicdebt.treas.gov/opd/opdm082008.pdf
6 http://www.treasuredirect.gov/NP/BPDLogin?application=np
7 http://finance.fortune.cnn.com/2011/04/25/sp-why-we-downgraded-our-u-s-outlook/
8 http://www.bing.com/apps/geography/search?domain=geography&loadExperience=1&q=us+gdp&qpvt=us+gdp http://www.bea.gov/newsreleases/national/gdp/gdpnewsrelease.htm
9 Eisner, *The Misunderstood Economy*, pp. 95-97
10 Benjamin M. Friedman, "US Fiscal Policy in the 1980s: Consequences of Large Budget Deficits

at Full Employment," *Debt and the Twin Deficits Debate*, p. 149

11 http://www.treasurydirect.gov/govt/reports/ir/ir_expense.htm

12 http://cboblog.cbo.gov/?p=555

13 Benjamin M. Friedman, "US Fiscal Policy in the 1980s: Consequences of Large Budget Deficits at Full Employment," *Debt and the Twin Deficits Debate*, p. 149

14 http://www.tcf.org/Publications/Basics/Balanced_Budget/index.html, Section How Bad is the Deficit, p. 3

15 http://www.auburn.edu/~johnspm/gloss/index.html?http://www.auburn.edu/~johnspm/gloss/money_stock.html

16 http://www.ustdrc.gov/reports/tdrc_ch3.pdf, page 85

17 http://www.whitehouse.gov/omb/budget/fy2008/pdf/spec.pdf, p 166

18 http://www.whitehouse.gov/omb/budget/fy2008/pdf/spec.pdf, p 234

19 Ibid. p.235

20 Robert Eisner, *The Misunderstood Economy: What Counts, and How to Count It* (Boston: Harvard Business School Press, 1994), p. 94

21 http://www.federalreserveboard.gov/faq

22 Ibid.
23 Ibid.
24 Ibid.
25 http://www.concordcoalition.org/federal_budget/030714fiscalresponsibilityrpt.pdf
26 Ibid.
27 https://www.cia.gov/library/publications/the-world-factbook/geos/co.html
28 http://www.whitehouse.gov/omb/budget/Analytical_Perspectives, econ_analyses document, page 15